Win at Greyhound Racing

Win at Greyhound Racing

H. Edwards Clarke

OLDCASTLE BOOKS · ENGLAND

1991

Oldcastle Books Ltd
18 Coleswood Road
Harpenden, Herts AL5 1EQ
England

Copyright © 1974 H. Edwards Clarke

Reprinted by Oldcastle Books 1988, 1989, 1991

First Published 1974 by Stanley Paul

British Library Cataloguing in Publication Data

Clarke, H. Edwards
Win at greyhound racing.
1. Gambling   2. Dog racing   3. Greyhounds
I. Title
798'.8   SF440
ISBN 0-948353-64-3

9 8 7 6 5 4 3

Printed by The Guernsey Press Co. Ltd.,
Guernsey, Channel Islands.

Contents

Photograph
Acknowledgements

The author and publisher are grateful to the following for permission to reproduce photographs of which they own the copyright:

Gerry Cranham
The Greyhound Racing Association
The Greyhound Racing Record, USA
The National Greyhound Racing Club Ltd
Syndication International
Wembley Stadium

Foreword

After forty-six years of greyhound racing at Wimbledon Stadium I recently retired from my post as racing director. Year after year, week after week and almost day after day I studied the techniques of greyhound racing both from the Stewards' Box and in the back rooms of Wimbledon. I was ceaselessly systematic in trying to understand the nature of greyhound racing and I began to consider that there could be no one more capable than I of writing a book on how to win at this sport. Indeed, I had every intention of writing such a book. But by the luck of fate, Mr H. Edwards Clarke paid me the compliment of sending me the typescript of *Win at Greyhound Racing* with an invitation to contribute an introduction.

He little knew what a service he was doing me. I might well have spent a great deal of effort writing a book on almost exactly the lines of his own, only to find he had beaten me to the post, not in a photofinish by but a wide margin.

I believe I have the right to judge what he says, even though I am now certain that I could not have produced such an extremely well argued and competent book myself. He has shown absolutely the right approach to winning at greyhound racing, and above all, emphasizes that most essential qualification, honest thinking.

I am sure too that I am right in thinking that anybody who reads carefully and digests the author's recommendations, will very significantly improve his chances of winning at greyhound racing.

Con Stevens

Publishers foreword to 1991 edition.

When "Win at Greyhound Racing" was first published in 1974 it was immediately recognised as the definitive guide to making the sport of Greyhound Racing both more enjoyable to watch and more profitable! Seventeen years later this still holds true. Indeed it is our experience through our associate company, Gamblers Book Services, from our own customers that nothing has been published in the interim to supersede this book.

In light of this we have declined to make wholesale alterations to the text in this new edition. The reader will note that some things have changed since 1974 – White City and Harringay are no more, metres have replaced yards and there have been some great greyhounds including Scurlogue Champ, Ballyregan Bob and Ravage Again who are worthy of inclusion in the "Hall of Fame". Since 1974 the Wimbledon method of grading races invented by Con Stevens, (A1, A2, A3 etc) has gained universal acceptance in Britain. In general the punter's job has been made easier with more informative racecards containing sectional times and positions at the quarters. All this information is useless, however, unless interpreted properly. This is where the step by step guidance and honest thinking urged by the author in this book still holds as true now as it ever did.

There are other books available on Greyhound Racing, including the Sporting Life Greyhound Annual and Greyhound Fact File, published by Ringpress and the excellent Timeform of Greyhound Racing – BAGSFORM – but if you buy just one book on the subject, you cannot go far wrong with "WIN AT GREYHOUND RACING"

Introduction

This book is written to honour a promise I made some months before his tragic death to a dear friend, the late Dr Richard Handley, founder of the British Greyhound Breeders Forum.

I can hear him now urging me to forget for once the pedigrees and the blue prints of pedigrees that were such an absorbing interest to us both, and to write a book fully descriptive of the greyhound racing scene for which our greyhounds were in fact designed. A work that would give as much weight to the conditions and setting of the stage on which they would be expected to perform as to the qualities required of the successful artistes themselves.

I can remember his argument that for each person absorbed and enthralled by the breeding side of the project there were countless thousands of greyhound racing fans to whom the thrill and excitement of greyhound racing was largely centred on the problem of How to Pick a Winner! Nor did I lose the point that he made – that by catering for their understandable demand I would be enlarging the army of happy punters from whom the next brigade of greyhound owners must necessarily draw its reserves.

In a work such as this it is hardly surprising that my list of indebtedness should be long.

I would like to pay tribute to Mr Underhill, the Secretary of the National Greyhound Racing Club Ltd, for his unfailing courtesy and co-operation on the many occasions I referred to him, and particularly for his invaluable comments on reading through the typescript.

My thanks to Commandant Fitzpatrick, the Secretary of the Irish Coursing Club, and Pat Holland of Bord na gCon, for the details of the greyhound racing scene in Ireland – still the source of the vast majority of the stars that grace our tracks.

A special word of thanks to Mildred Hopkins of *The Greyhound Racing Record* without whose assistance so promptly and generously afforded me it would have been impossible even to do broad justice to the American scene let alone to the American stars of the Hall of Fame.

I am indebted to my daughter Jill for providing the diagrammatic line drawings which I feel contribute so effectively to a better understanding of the text.

I would also like to add my personal appreciation, with that of my publishers, to my secretary, Edna King, for her patience and skill in translating an almost illegible manuscript into a neat and eminently presentable typescript.

Finally I offer this book, with all its imperfections and shortcomings, to those thousands who find their pleasure in 'Going to the Dogs'. If it adds to their pleasure and maybe even to their profit, I shall be doubly rewarded for I will have had the inner satisfaction too of not failing in a promise to a friend.

1

The Origin of Greyhound Racing

When at the Welsh Harp, Hendon, one September afternoon in 1876 Mr Leary sent six greyhounds racing after his mechanically propelled hare, little could he have thought that he was sowing the seeds of a sport that ultimately, with some eight million fans, was destined to become second only to football as the largest spectator sport in Britain. The reason the sport did not catch on in nineteenth-century England is probably that the mechanical hare was driven over a straight course. Moreover it had to compete with coursing which was then in its heyday.

In the United States, however, the infinitely greater excitement and potential of racing greyhounds round a circular or oval track had exercised the inventive brain of Owen Patrick Smith for some years, and the young engineer had already taken out several patents on various racing devices and equipment. Even in the USA greyhound racing did not make an immediate popular appeal, as is shown by the series of his financially distressing earlier promotions.

By 1919, however, Smith had perfected his mechanical hare and successfully demonstrated it at his first track at Emeryville, California. Thereafter such names as Tulsa, Hialeah, St Petersburg, Biscayne, Flagler, Multnomah, Wonderland, Taunton, Raynham, Caliente serve almost as milestones in greyhound racing's popular progress across the United States. So much so that with fourteen million fans greyhound racing is now the seventh ranking spectator sport in that country.

Smith's friend Charles Munn, quick to appreciate the appeal of the project, brought the patents to the United Kingdom and with Brigadier-General A. C. Critchley and Major L. Lyne Dixon formed a company, The Greyhound Racing Association, with a capital of £14 000 to exploit the sporting and financial potential of greyhound racing. The story of their efforts reads almost like a Cinderella, rags-to-riches fairy tale. They enlisted the co-operation of William Gentle who in 1926 agreed to construct the first greyhound racing stadium on his property at Belle Vue, Manchester.

That the first greyhound racing meeting in England was staged there on the night of 24 July 1926 is history now, as is the fact that the first programme consisted of three races at 440 yards, two at 550 and one hurdle race at 440 yards. The name of the winner of the first greyhound race in Britain, Mistley, has also gone down in sporting history, along, of course, with that of Charming Nell, the little black bitch that won that race at the Welsh Harp in 1876!

The first night attracted a meagre crowd of some 1700. As it resulted in a loss of £50 it is fair to deduce that in show business parlance a large proportion of these represented 'paper'. The second night did little better, but almost miraculously the tide changed. The sporting interests of the North West somehow or other were aroused and thereafter the turnstiles never stopped clicking. At the next meeting 16 000 paid for admission and far from the attendances falling as the novelty wore off, the reverse was the case.

When the first eleven weeks' season concluded at Belle Vue on the night of 9 October 1926 some thirty-seven meetings had attracted an average attendance of eleven thousand. Greyhound racing had won its first battle and henceforth it developed into a victorious campaign. In less than a year the private company that Brigadier-General Critchley, Charles Munn and William Gentle had formed, had become a public company, Greyhound Racing Association Limited.

Just as O. P. Smith's success at Hialeah inspired others to

extend and promote the sport in the States, so too it spread in England and by April 1927 – within six months – Liverpool had its track. By midsummer London had 'gone to the Dogs' and 25 June 1927 saw the opening night at the White City. Before another year was out tracks had opened at Harringay, Wembley and Wimbledon, and in due course in most of the major cities throughout the country. The Dogs – greyhound racing – had arrived to take their place in the British sporting scene.

In Ireland the Dogs made just as impelling an appeal. In April 1927 a track was opened at Celtic Park, Belfast. Not to be outdone Dublin opened its Shelbourne Park on Easter Monday, 14 May 1927. Remarkably, although it had taken greyhound racing three to four years to cross the Atlantic from the States, it took less than one year to reach Australia where the track at Harold Park, Glebe, inaugurated greyhound racing on 28 May 1927!

Looking back at the phenomenal growth of greyhound racing not only in the United Kingdom and the States but also in Australia, Spain and more recently Italy and Denmark, one may well seek the reasons both for the extent and nature of its appeal. Unquestionably the location of tracks within or adjacent to the large urban areas – readily accessible to the vast numbers of town and city dwellers – was a potent factor in its popularity. So too was the decision to stage greyhound racing in the evening. Hitherto the great mass of the country's working population had been denied, by their hours of work, any active interest in horse racing save for reading the columns of the Racing Press and staking their 'tanners' with the local pub bookie.

The Dogs altered all that. For the first time the British public found they could get home from work, have their meal, get a bus or Tube to their local track and enjoy the brilliant, exciting spectacle of gaily-jacketed greyhounds racing round a floodlit track. Moreover, for the first time the British public found they had the right and freedom to have a cash bet on their sporting fancy, either with the Tote or the bookmaker, without the humiliating feeling that they were doing something underhand, squalid or illegal.

As the sport became more popular and the tracks became more prosperous, the more enlightened concerns ploughed back a fair proportion of their profits into the business. Consequently, such amenities as the stands, bars, restaurants, Tote booths, etc., were both enlarged and improved, to the extent that it was not long before the ordinary man soon found he could safely bring his wife or girl friend for a most enjoyable evening at the Dogs.

These reasons for the appeal and popularity of greyhound racing, the accessibility of its stadia, the convenience of its hours, the comforts of its amenities, can only be appreciated against the background of what the Turf then had to offer. For decades Saturday-afternoon racegoers had been fenced off and herded almost like cattle in draughty ill-sited areas of the Silver Ring, where they were able to see neither the start nor the finish, and where there was little scope and less comfort even to sit down. As for the victuals – stale sandwiches and wishy-washy tea – they made a mockery of the very word 'refreshments'! Small wonder then that, quite apart from the relative merits of the sport itself, the amenities provided by such tracks as White City, Wembley, Wimbledon and Walthamstow, were a potent factor in drawing crowds to greyhound racing.

But it is, I feel, unquestionable that any sport, any form of entertainment, must have something other than such material inducements if it is to survive the trends and fashions and often fickle popular whims.

There are those who argue that the facility for betting is the main, and indeed the sole, reason for the appeal and popularity of greyhound racing. Personally I doubt if this is so. Since the Betting and Gaming Act of 1960 the British public have not been short of betting media, whether football pools, bingo, the casinos or the ubiquitous betting shops. No one would seek to deny that greyhound racing is primarily a betting sport but that is no reason to moralize against it. So too is horse racing and football. To those who regard all betting as an indication of a weakening of the moral fibre, it is fair to remark that the whole climate of both private and public opinion in regard to betting has changed fundamentally in the past decade.

Logically one can argue that the Government itself has been in the betting business ever since it authorized the Postmaster-General to lay odds of £150 to 20p or £500 to 25p that he would not lose the registered letter you entrust to the Post Office! The Government itself is now patently in the betting business as it openly invites the public to buy its Premium Bonds at £1 apiece and as there are 952 million Bonds in each draw it effectively lays you odds of 10360-1 against winning a prize of any amount.

The Government's most important and far-reaching change of heart was of course its enactment in 1960 of the Betting and Gaming Act which legalized cash betting and the setting up of betting shops and casinos. The broad truth therefore is that the Government has recognized that betting in some form or other is an inseparable part of our lives. There is hardly a citizen who does not enter into some form of betting transaction. He may bet with an insurance company, for instance, that his car will not crash, that his house will not be burned down, or that he will not die within a specified period.

The Stock Exchange has long defended its existence on the score that it ensures an adequate flow of capital for joint-stock companies. But this is true only of initial invitations to the public for concerns going public or Rights Issues for established concerns seeking to expand. It is as invalid as it is misleading to argue that the sale by A of 1000 ICI shares of £1 nominal value to B for £3, can in any way make a contribution to the financial needs of that company.

With the benefit of hindsight no one can say that all the consequences of the 1960 legislation were either politically prudent or socially desirable, but at least what had amounted to invidious class discrimination was removed. The legislation at least eliminated the hypocrisy that allowed a man to bet freely provided he was wealthy or 'creditable' enough to have an account with a bookmaker, but denied the same liberty to his less fortunate, less affluent brother unless he was prepared to break the law and bet with some street-corner bookie's runner!

In this new legal climate it is difficult to understand the moral stigma that some people attach to betting; those who regard it as a social or moral evil. Admittedly, one does not have to be a welfare worker to appreciate the social misery that betting beyond one's means, gambling to excess, can cause.

But the same can be said of many of the pleasures of life if carried to *excess*. Eating to excess – gluttony – and smoking to excess can cause considerable personal misery. Drinking to excess – drunkenness – can cause not only personal misery but untold social misery and squalor. Vitamin tablets, sleeping pills, when taken to excess, out of their medical context, can exact their toll of human suffering. So too can *betting to excess*.

The moral and social evil lies in the excess, in the lack of self-control. As regards betting there is still an age-old, golden rule that is as true today as ever it was – 'never bet more than you can cheerfully afford to lose'. The operative word needless to say is *cheerfully*.

By this standard a man paying surtax on his income would be justified in betting £20 or more on the grounds that if he lost, although he might not relish it, at least it would not basically affect his resources or his cheerfulness. An old age pensioner who wagered his total pension would be culpable because it would not be an inconsiderable proportion of his resources, and as such he could hardly be expected to suffer such a loss cheerfully.

The average man who keeps this in mind and abides by this adage when he takes his wife or girl friend greyhound racing is not likely to come to much harm. If he were to go into the West End and have a drink before a theatre or cinema and a meal afterwards he would not expect it to cost him nothing. In fact he would have at the back of his mind the limit he was prepared to spend – just how much the night was worth.

The excitement and thrill of watching well-bred animals, horses or dogs, contesting a close-run race is sufficient entertainment for many people, especially if they have bred, reared or trained them.

But for an infinitely greater number of people, that thrill is magnified by having a small stake on your opinion of the result of that race. In much the same way, a game of whist, bridge or poker is enlivened by some element of gain or loss, no matter how small. It is significant that a small stake increases the concentration and you do not then hear the fatuous query 'What are trumps, my dear?' With the increased concentration there comes increased pleasure. So too with a flutter on the Dogs.

There is reason to believe that most regular greyhound racing fans do their sums on similar lines and take into account the cost of admission, drinks, the meal, and a few bets. The night out will then be comparable with a theatre or dinner outing. If he is at all lucky or if he has added the pleasure of study to his effort and has won on a race or two, then the total cost will be reduced accordingly. Conceivably, the night out may have cost him nothing! At the worst he will merely have spent what he might on an alternative night out.

Against such a background of self-control and moderation it is difficult to appreciate the moral or social evils that the more pessimistic and narrow moralists would attach to betting on the Dogs.

But if the basic reason for the phenomenal growth of greyhound racing is not to be found in such material factors as its admirable accessibility and amenities, and if it is not to be found in the allure of its betting facilities, then one may well ask where its appeal lies.

To beg the question I have no doubt that people go greyhound racing consistently because they thoroughly enjoy it. Which in turn leads to the question, why do they enjoy greyhound racing? For my part I have no doubt that the answer simply is that it affords people the thrill of pitting their judgement of the ability of the greyhounds against the judgement of their fellows. Primarily against the judgement of the man who has set the problem, who has compiled the card, the Racing Manager; and then against the judgement of the bookmakers who are prepared to advertise their estimate of the merits and chances of the various competitors in the shape of odds on their betting boards.

Proof of the view that the fascination and appeal of greyhound racing lies in the stimulation of anticipation – what will happen in a race – and in the later argument over what has happened in a race, can be found in the frequency with which one hears the phrase 'what did I tell you?' which often arises from little knots of fans.

The object of this book will be to convince and encourage you that the thrill of greyhound racing consists of setting not merely your views and opinions but also the weight of your concentrated study of a race card, against such professionals as the Racing Manager and the bookmaker – and moreover to your profit!

2

The Shape of
Greyhound Racing

But with popularity came other problems. The phenomenal success of greyhound racing almost proved its own undoing. Projects sprang up all over the country with almost mushroom-like rapidity. Appeals were made to the public for financial support, so honey-worded that one might have been forgiven for believing that shares in a greyhound racing company were almost equivalent to a licence to print one's own money.

Quite apart from the irresponsible blandishments of the promoters of many of the new companies, the tracks which they operated in many cases did scant credit to the new sport. All the old tricks and stunts pulled in the shady days of horse racing found new life in the Dogs. It was soon apparent that there must be some form of control if the malpractices of these mushroom tracks were not to blacken the reputation and popularity of the honest, well-managed ones.

As early as 1928 it became clear that if the sport were to continue to prosper and maintain a responsible public image, it must have an authoritative controlling body which would administer greyhound racing in much the same way as the Jockey Club controlled horse racing.

Accordingly the various interests got together and it was decided that as there were two distinct interests to be safeguarded, that is, the track owners and the general sporting public, these would best be served by two separate bodies, the National Greyhound Racing Society and the National Greyhound Racing Club.

The National Greyhound Racing Society of Great Britain Limited was the federation of those companies which owned race-courses licensed by the National Greyhound Racing Club. Its first object was not unnaturally to protect the business interests of greyhound racing. It operated through a Council drawn from its own members and to which various regional committees reported with their recommendations for certain action on general matters of policy.

It acted as the spokesman for greyhound racing when its views had, for instance, to be put to the Government, the Press, the BBC or the bookmakers' representatives. On the all-important matter of security it fell to the National Greyhound Racing Society to take effective action to prevent malpractices or misdemeanours likely to tarnish the sport's reputation. The National Greyhound Racing Society in short was the sport's administrative body, the 'Civil Service' of greyhound racing.

The National Greyhound Racing Club, as the body responsible for the general conduct of racing, naturally came more into the public eye than the National Greyhound Racing Society. Constitutionally, it acted through a body of public stewards who had no financial interests in greyhound racing management. Its main objects were to protect the public's interest in greyhound racing by framing a set of rules by reference to which its several autonomous and financially independent members would be expected to conduct themselves. It is a tribute to their work that the Rules framed in 1928 are still basically those in force today, and there is evidence for the view that the National Greyhound Racing Club Rules for greyhound racing did what the Queensberry Rules have done for boxing.

Briefly, the National Greyhound Racing Club served greyhound racing in much the same way as the Jockey Club served the Turf.

But by the 1970s the wind of change was beginning to make itself felt. Just as in other spheres of political, social and sporting life, groups, factions and parties were pressing for more independence from the central authority and a greater say in the conduct of their own affairs, so too in greyhound racing. It is to the credit of the greyhound racing 'establishment' that it recognized and accepted these new trends and in March 1972 gave effect to a root-and-branch reorganization of its administrative functions which was proof positive of its ability and desire to move with the times.

Throughout the life of greyhound racing there had developed a number of bodies and associations, each one formed to foster, develop and protect its particular interest, be it training, breeding, betting or ownership. For example, The Greyhound Trainers Association, The Greyhound Breeders Forum, The Society of Greyhound Veterinarians, The National Association of Bookmakers and The Greyhound Council of Great Britain. Up to 1972 none of these bodies (although their purpose established their sincere interest in the sport of greyhound racing) had had a voice in the Councils of the NGRC or the NGRS.

It was to alleviate this need and to be seen to move with the times that in March 1972 the following root-and-branch reorganization of the constitution of the governing bodies of greyhound racing was effected.

The new step in the reorganization was the replacement of the two bodies – the National Greyhound Racing Society and the National Greyhound Racing Club – by a new company, the National Greyhound Racing Club Limited which had at its head a General Committee which was to operate through two main divisions, a Racing Committee and a Policy Committee, with provision for a third division, a Liaison Committee. See Figure 1 on page 24.

At the risk of over-simplification, it would be fair to say that their functions and spheres of influence were as follows:

General Committee

To control the finances of the Club.

To appoint senior staff.

To receive the annual reports of the Racing, Policy and Liaison Committees and thereby oversee general policy.

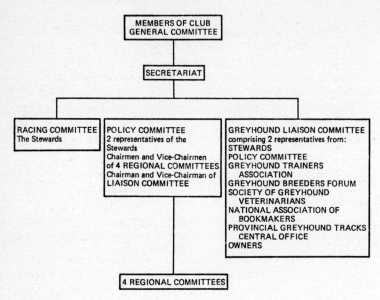

```
                    ┌─────────────────────┐
                    │  MEMBERS OF CLUB     │
                    │  GENERAL COMMITTEE   │
                    └─────────────────────┘
                              │
                        ┌───────────┐
                        │ SECRETARIAT │
                        └───────────┘
                              │
    ┌────────────────┬────────┴──────────────────────┐
```

| RACING COMMITTEE
The Stewards | POLICY COMMITTEE
2 representatives of the
Stewards
Chairmen and Vice-Chairmen
of 4 REGIONAL COMMITTEES
Chairman and Vice-Chairman of
LIAISON COMMITTEE | GREYHOUND LIAISON COMMITTEE
comprising 2 representatives from:
STEWARDS
POLICY COMMITTEE
GREYHOUND TRAINERS
  ASSOCIATION
GREYHOUND BREEDERS FORUM
SOCIETY OF GREYHOUND
  VETERINARIANS
NATIONAL ASSOCIATION OF
  BOOKMAKERS
PROVINCIAL GREYHOUND TRACKS
  CENTRAL OFFICE
OWNERS |

```
                    ┌─────────────────────┐
                    │ 4 REGIONAL COMMITTEES │
                    └─────────────────────┘
```

Figure 1

Racing Committee

To exercise complete supervision and control of the *racing matters* at its forty odd licensed tracks.

Policy Committee

To exercise authority in all non racing *business* matters, and to talk as greyhound racing's negotiating body with the Government, the Press, television and the bookmakers.

Liaison Committee

To discuss mutual problems affecting the sport and to submit recommendations to the Racing and Policy Committees.

The appointment of the Liaison Committee represented the

major change in the constitution of greyhound racing. To the extent that it gave a voice for the first time to the other parties interested in the greyhound itself and all aspects of its husbandry, then it represented the first yielding to the wind of change.

For the first time the views and opinions of outside associations and interests were able to express themselves not merely in the corridors of power but in the chambers of authority by making their recommendations to the Racing and Policy Committee. The extent to which the new body, the National Greyhound Racing Club Limited, aspires to the position of a national board representing the whole of the greyhound racing industry, can be judged from the inclusion in the Liaison Committee of two members from the Provincial Greyhound Tracks Central Office, which represents those independent tracks that operate outside the orbit of the NGRC.

In this connection it would be as easy as it is misleading to suggest that all the tracks operating greyhound racing throughout the country are licensed by the NGRC or are doing so in accordance with NGRC rules. There are no fewer than sixty-six tracks operating independently of the NGRC some of which have standards of spectator amenity, as well as standards of security and straight running and first-class presentation of the sport, that are little if anything short of the major NGRC tracks.

Prior to 1972, however well organized the *horizontal* strata of the industry may have been, there was nevertheless a *vertical* split which separated those tracks licensed by and subscribing to the rules of the NGRC and those other tracks which promoted greyhound racing independently of the central body. The fact that such 'independents' as Ipswich, Cambridge and Halifax have agreed to race under NGRC rules and that others have becom members of the Provincial Tracks Federation and therefore affiliated to the NGRC is proof of the industry's growing desire to march forward under one banner.

By way of explanation it may be pertinent to add that the basic distinction between the NGRC and independent tracks is not to be found in the quality of the sport nor in the amenities provided, but in the approach to the treatment of the greyhounds themselves.

It is no overstatement to say that the closed kennel system has always been the lynchpin of those tracks operating under NGRC Rules. Under this system the track kennels all the dogs that are to participate in its graded races. In some cases, Wembley for instance, the track had its own range of kennels in the stadium precincts itself; kennels which were under the control and management of Track Trainers with an appropriate quota of head lads, kennel boys and girls. Other tracks like White City, Harringay and Wimbledon chose to kennel their dogs outside London and transported them each night to the track from their establishments at Northaw or Burhill.

It was therefore essential to greyhound racing that the Racing Manager of NGRC tracks compiled his race card for the various graded races from the dogs in the ranges of the track's licensed trainers. The main advantage of such a system was the certain and immediate availability of sufficient and suitable dogs to make up a full card.

The other advantage claimed for the closed kennel system was the all-important one of security. In the early free-for-all days before the formation of the NGRC some of the mushroom tracks had operated in a way that did scant credit to the new sport. The answer to this shady skulduggery was sought in stipulating that the owners of all dogs should entrust them to the strict custody and control of the track itself, and that they be housed in a range of kennels operated by the track's own employees. In this way the closed kennel system was born.

In fact in the very early days of the sport some tracks favoured an even tighter closed kennel system. On such tracks as Salford and Middlesborough for instance, all the greyhounds in the kennels were the property of the track itself. That this never became common practice was due to the fact that it cut at one of the roots of greyhound racing's greatest appeals – the right and pride of individual ownership!

To own a racehorse is probably one of the most common pipe dreams of any hopeful punter. But if such ambitions are inevitably beyond his compass, the Dogs – as many thousands will aver – at least allow the man of quite modest means to indulge the pride of possession of a racing animal. Some tracks, anxious to cater for this popular urge and to facilitate individual ownership conceived the idea of buying greyhounds and leasing them out to their patrons, who thereafter were responsible for them. So admirably did this scheme meet the deep-rooted desire to own a dog that it became, and still is, common practice in tracks as widespread as London (White City), Manchester (Belle Vue), Edinburgh and Southend, to mention but a few.

Until quite recently the only variation of the closed kennel system was in the case of Open Races which, as their name indicates, were open to all greyhounds no matter where they were kennelled. Even then the rules governing the entry for such races normally stipulated that the visiting greyhounds must be kennelled and examined in the official range for at least two hours before the commencement of the meeting.

Whatever criticisms are now made of a system whose origins trace back some forty-five years, at least it is certain that it served a useful purpose in the formative years of a rapidly expanding business. Without the resources of the tracks' own kennels, which in some cases harboured as many as 200 dogs, it would have been virtually impossible for most tracks consistently to compile cards of eight races with six entries in each. These entries, moreover, could be so closely graded and matched that in many cases there was less than 0·30 of a second between the contestants in each race.

But a system that was beneficial in the early and formative years of a business is not necessarily good for all time. The freedom-loving spirit of the seventies that was in revolt against the restraints and restrictions in political and social walks of life, inevitably made itself felt in the greyhound racing sphere. The closed kennel system began to be seen as an exclusive, almost monopolistic, instrument of the 'establishment's' authority. As such it became the target for attack.

It says much for the commonsense and wisdom of that 'establishment' that it was broadminded and indeed flexible enough to agree to variations and concessions in a system that had operated on the whole effectively for over forty years in much the same way as they had agreed to modifications of the constitutional framework of the N G R C. It is against this background that the significance of the following major modifications of the past five years can best be viewed.

The first departure from the strict closed kennel system was the introduction of the C Licence System. Under this scheme the NGRC were prepared to issue licences to certain persons to train greyhounds in family ownership, i.e. in the ownership of the wife or husband or married daughter. Greyhounds within this family group could be trained and entered for graded races at courses specified by the Stewards. Such tracks as Oxford and Swindon have accepted dogs trained under C licences for several years.

It is probably no overstatement to say that the success of the C licence system encouraged the NGRC to be even more adventurous and depart even further from the closed kennel system by inaugurating the dispersed kennel system.

Under this system the race-course engaged a private trainer to train greyhounds for graded races. The fact that the trainer had a contract with the track to supply so many dogs for each meeting gave rise to the name the *contract* kennel system. As, however, the distinctive feature of the system is its physical separation from the track, and the trainer is no longer an employee of the track – then clearly the phrase *dispersed* kennel system is the more apt.

By the adoption of the dispersed kennel system greyhound racing in the United Kingdom fell into line with the pattern adopted by the USA from the inception of the sport. Under their traditional system a greyhound owner would not be allowed to race a dog at, say, the Biscayne track – with its franchise to hold a specified maximum of meetings in its ninety-day season – unless he first leased it to one of the training kennels, say, Happy Stutz's, which had been granted a 'booking' or contract by Biscayne to supply a minimum of thirty greyhounds for racing and up to a required standard.

It is arguable that these root-and-branch changes in the shape of greyhound racing were as much brought about by the prevalent rationalization of the greyhound racing industry as the desire to broaden its outlook and extend more liberty to trainers. In an era of inflation and rising prices, of building boom and consequent land shortage, it was inevitable that many greyhound racing stadia that owned large areas of land were sought after by the take-over development tycoons. For many tracks the most effective defence against such take-overs was to be found in a more up-to-date, efficient and profitable management of the business of greyhound racing.

It is against this background of inflation, of land shortage, of take-over projects, that the adoption of the dispersed kennel system must be viewed. In this perspective the hiving-off of a track's heavy commitments, the liquidation of its liability to maintain its own ranges of kennels by the appointment of contract trainers, can be viewed as a logical and prudent project of rationalization. That its adoption by almost half of the NGRC tracks has been instrumental in enabling greyhound racing to face the financial and economic challenge of the property tycoons is undeniable.

The old argument of security that sustained the closed kennel system has been proved to be invalid. If the country's criminal element are capable of organizing robbery on the scale of the Great Train Robbery and of robbing the vaults of our largest banks, no kennel system of any kind is going to prevent their skulduggery if they wish to apply their warped ingenuity to any sport.

So much then for the origin and shape of greyhound racing, for the factors which over the years have been responsible for the transformation of what was once regarded as an overnight craze, or at best a seven-days wonder, into the second largest spectator sport in Britain.

That a knowledge of this background will not *of itself* assist one's quest for winners is beyond dispute. On the other hand in the study of any subject – and I urge that the finding of winners at greyhound racing does involve intense study as the following chapters will bear out – it is invariably sound practice to acquire a broad knowledge of the framework of the game which poses the problems you are hoping profitably to solve. Or in chess terms to know the range of the board and the rules for deploying the pieces.

At the outset may I stress again that the aim of this book is to assist readers to make greyhound racing pay. That it is possible to convert an enjoyable form of entertainment into a profitable or at least a consistently self-supporting pastime, brooks no denial. There are several hundreds of racegoers who can vouchsafe this statement, but all of them will stress that success at greyhound racing – as in many other walks of life – demands both study and concentration.

Even the most whimsical, fanciful racegoer, who has his flutter for no more impelling reason than that he fancies a dog, or because it is in a particular trap, or even because it has evacuated on parade – even these punters can back winners. Occasionally they have a run of luck and are in pocket for two or three meetings, but it offends common sense to believe that this haphazard 'animated roulette' attitude can be consistently profitable.

All the evidence goes to show that those consistently successful at greyhound racing have a capacity for critical and analytical judgement. That this ability can be acquired is beyond dispute. It will be my aim in the following chapters to pinpoint and consider those aspects, a working knowledge of which, experience has proved, point the way to profitable greyhound racing.

1 The assessment of the characteristics and calibre, traits and talents, vices and virtues of the dogs themselves.

2 The ability to read a race, i.e. to identify and assess those happenings in a race that may prevent a dog from winning by denying it the opportunity of giving of its best.

3 The ability to assess the effect of the contours and conditions of the track itself (the stage on which it must perform) on a dog's performance.

Finally, and probably most important of all:

4 The ability to assess and assimilate 'form' – to evaluate from a dog's previous performances its prospects of winning a particular race.

3

How to Assess a Greyhound

The student of greyhound racing has much in common with the chess player. Just as the latter must learn to recognize the particular capabilities of his 'pieces' and the circumstances in which they can be utilized – the speed and power of his Queen, the leap-frogging ability of his Knight – so too must the student of greyhound racing learn to recognize the particular talent of his pieces and how his fast trappers, railers and wide runners can best exploit their gifts.

In this chapter, therefore, I propose to consider the various characteristics of a racing greyhound and to classify them for the purpose of simplifying an assessment of their ability or likelihood of winning a particular race.

The first basic truth that becomes apparent to students of greyhound racing is that 'the race is not always to the swift'. If greyhound racing were conducted over a straight track of 400, 525, 550, 700 yards – as was the original Welsh Harp experiment – it would not last a week. For the simple reason that it would lack the interest of variety as the fastest dog would win consistently.

Greyhound racing is an interesting, exciting sport simply because it is staged on an oval track with three, four, five, six or more bends to be negotiated. It is the jockeying for position, the inevitable bumping and baulking, going into and coming out of the bends, that adds the variety and thrill which has made greyhound racing so universally popular both as a spectacle and as a betting medium.

Oddly enough speed or pace in the conventional sense is not the all-important quality in a track greyhound. There are only two aspects of a race in which speed, in the sense of covering a distance between two points in the shortest time, can be exploited. First, in the dash from the traps to the first bend, which even on the largest track, for example, Hackney, Walthamstow, Wimbledon, is seldom more than 115 yards. Second, in the back-straight – coming out of the second to the third bend – which again seldom exceeds 115 yards.

But one has only to look at the scale design of any large track – the White City or Wembley – to appreciate that the major part of any race comprises the circumference of a circle, or to be more exact, of two terminal *semi*-circles. At the White City, for instance, the circumference of these two semi-circles comprise no less than 230 yards of the total 525 yard trip. At Wembley it is some 210 yards.

The ability to negotiate bends, to run the curves of a track faster than one's rivals – this is what greyhound racing is all about! The first lesson to be learned from this basic truth is that the ability to run a curve is a more important quality than sheer speed. Such an ability is largely dependent upon such factors as balance, muscular control and coordination. It has been said with some truth that the difference between a track greyhound and an Irish park coursing greyhound is the same as that between a Dirt Track motorcyclist and a T.T. or Grand Prix performer.

The next logical distinction in assessing the capabilities of a racing greyhound is essentially one of degree – the extent to which a dog can run a curve without losing too much ground by dint of *covering* too much ground! Out of this distinction there derive two types of dog, commonly referred to as railers and wide runners. The terms are self-explanatory. The railer takes the shortest way round the curve, running as close to the fence as possible. The wide runner through lack of balance or muscular control is unable to counter the centrifugal force which pushes it off wide from the inner rail and sends it racing off in the middle of the track.

On the other hand, attributing wide running purely to physical and muscular factors may well be an undue simplification of the issue; *mental* urges affect the issue. In the case of an outside hare there are dogs which instinctively run out towards the hare in their primitive natural desire to catch it. This trait not infrequently manifests itself in greyhounds who are not schooled for greyhound racing until they are mature, or after they have had a season or two coursing their natural quarry in the open.

Whatever the reason, the railer takes the shortest route by hugging the rails whereas the wide runner takes the longer route but by virtue of its width has more scope to stretch out freely and thereby compensate a little for taking the longer trip.

To be logical one should also take into account the middle track runners. The middle track is sometimes adopted by choice but frequently by runners in traps 4 and 5 who are not clear at the first bend and have to 'go overland' on the outside of the faster trapping group. For those of a statistical turn of mind it has been calculated that if the tight railer, running one foot from the rail, covers 525 yards at White City, then the middle track runner, maintaining a uniform course of 6 feet off the rail, covers 531 yards, while the wide runner racing 10 feet off the rail covers some 535 yards. One has but to realize that as Racing Managers conventionally make an allowance of 0·06 seconds for each length or yard, then the advantage of any animal taking the shortest route round the oval course would appear to transcend all other considerations. Certainly few, if any, wide runners are beaten by more than their 'excess' trip.

But for those who regard railing as all-important the question has but to be posed as to what happens when the tight railer also happens to be a slow trapper. Surely there is no sight more common, or indeed more frustrating, than to see a greyhound sticking like a leech to the rails all the way round but unable to get through because two or three others have come over to the rails by dint of quicker trapping or superior early pace, and are thereby presenting it with an impenetrable close-up view of their backsides. There has probably been much money lost at greyhound racing by the inability to appreciate that a slow trapping railer is the most expensive combination in the game!

But if fast trapping and early pace transcend the ability to rail it is but logical to consider these faculties in some depth. The breeder, rearer or trainer who can impart the ability to trap smartly to his charges will be well on the way to affluence. It may be that the really brilliant box hitters, like Fine Jubilee, Ballynennan Moon and Magna Hasty were born with the gift and certainly some puppies take to it naturally. Patient schooling may have something to do with it but basically it seems to be a natural gift.

The design of starting boxes nowadays has done a lot to iron out any technical hindrances – the natural upcurve of the front tends to avoid the risk of dogs' feet going up with the traps. But at least one private trainer I know has achieved more than normal success by schooling his puppies with an older fast trapper in special traps with glass divisions so that the puppies can watch the antics of the old 'un as he literally 'gets down' to his job of hitting the box.

I for one am inclined to think that many of the really brilliant box hitters – the ones that in the vernacular are away before the lid goes up – use their ears to help them on their way. Certainly I have watched them in the box cocking their ears for what may well be the first mechanical click intimating that the traps are about to spring.

But whatever views there may be as to whether fast trapping can be instilled there can be no argument that the faculty of early pace, the ability of getting quickly into one's stride is a gift. Moreover it is one of the most valuable attributes of any racing greyhound. One has but to stand some 50 yards ahead of the traps with a stopwatch and time the foremost dog to the first bend in each race to appreciate that the gulf between bottom grade and top grade largely begins here.

The vital importance of early pace, especially where it is allied (as it is so often, but not always) with fast trapping, is that it assures a clear run into and round the first bend. From that point onwards the dog is virtually on a solo trial. There can be no excuses, no complaints that it could not get through, that it was baulked or chopped off. It has set the pace with a clear run thanks to its early pace and if it cannot sustain the trip then a better dog has beaten it.

There are those who associate fast trapping and especially early pace with an inability to sustain the gallop; in other words to regard it as the attribute of the pure sprinter type whose limit is about 440 yards. This is almost certainly a fallacy that derives from the fact that all sprinters are necessarily fast trappers and necessarily have early pace. It stands to reason that over a course of 300 to 400 yards there is mighty little opportunity to overcome an initial deficit of three to four lengths, certainly against top class opposition.

But because all sprinters are fast trappers with early pace, it does not follow that all fast trappers with early pace are sprinters. Some of our very greatest Cesarewitch and indeed St Leger winners were endowed with sufficient early pace to win top class Opens over 500 yards.

As an insurance against 'bad luck' the ability to be clear at the first bend is also important in a 600 yard race. It is only of less relative importance than in a shorter race in that the longer the distance the more the field strings out into single file and forms a less obstructive block to pass.

In his attempts to assess the relative merits of the various greyhounds at his local track I doubt whether any student of greyhound racing could be better advised than to proceed first and foremost on a study and record of their early pace. If he records on his race cards their stopwatch times, first time over the winning line or to the first bend, he will be well on the way to assessing one of the most important of all racing characteristics and one that will pay him useful dividends.

Some progressive tracks – Wimbledon for instance – actually incorporate the times from the traps to the first crossing of the winning line on their official race cards and trail sheets. They call them Starting times which is probably as good a nomenclature as any for the dual facility – fast trapping and early pace.

In the longer distance races, say those of 650 to 700 yards, the aspirant assessor should be on the look out for the dog which is being asked to tackle a distance which is beyond him. With the present vogue for distance races this is by no means uncommon. In fact the demand is so great that tracks not infrequently offer incentives such as higher prize money to urge owners to race over the longer distances.

In many instances, especially with puppies, it is beyond their natural compass. The alert student will make a note of the dog that leads for a long part of the trip and then patently fades over the last 100 yards. That dog may well be very good value for money the next time he is graded for a 525 race.

A simple deduction? Yes, but so often it is overlooked. Perhaps just as frequently as the running which is really the reverse side of the coin – the dog that is beaten four to five lengths in a 525 yard race, which is nevertheless first at the pick up, i.e. some 75 yards further ahead. These are the dogs to back when first they run over distances longer than 525 yards. The alert assessor of such faculties will have had valuable notice of its ability to stay on.

There can be few racing fans who have not had cause to curse the dog which is beaten a length by a winner in, say, 29·36 seconds and which when dropped in class and made favourite in his next race still runs a short head second to a winner in 29·90. The astute race reader will have identified it as a 'chaser'.

Basically the trouble is as deeprooted as it is ineradicable. The dog is not zealous enough really to chase the hare in the sense of wanting to possess it. Possibly the cause is boredom or just sheer lack of interest in an ever elusive quarry. All it does is to ga'lop and to match strides with the fastest of its fellows. Once it heads them the game is over as far as it is concerned and it then relaxes and lets the other dog take over the lead. The chaser in short plays a game of rather spiritless Follow My Leader.

Just what can be done about this type of runner? The answer frankly is little or nothing. Such greyhounds seldom, if ever, win a race unless by chance they misjudge their play and happen to edge in front at the winning line. They may not even finish second often enough to justify backing them for a place in most of their races – though certainly often enough to warrant putting them in a forecast with a well considered 'selection'.

There is another type of greyhound that the intelligent race reader will be anxious to identify as soon as possible – certainly before the Racing Manager. I refer of course to the dog that is prone to turn his head or to interfere with his rivals. The rules stipulate that such an interferer should be disqualified. The would-be aspirant to greyhound expertise, however, might well ask himself just why he should bother about the fighter or the potential fighter if it is the Racing Manager's job to sort it out. The answer of course is that there are degrees of interference that fall short of fighting but which still affect the result of a true run race.

There is every reason why a fan anxious to make his greyhound racing pay should identify greyhounds with interfering tendencies as soon as possible. Not only do fighters have no wish to go to the front themselves but they clearly prevent or discourage other runners from so doing. If the race reader's researches have indicated that there is one runner which he considers suspect for interfering tendencies, the odds are that it is not going to be a clean run race. If the layers have overlooked this then the odds on offer may well be completely false and bear out the wisdom of the adage that a race with a possible delinquent therein is always a poor betting medium.

The problem of the fighter is one that has beset greyhound racing from its earliest days. By and large it is surprising that there are so few. As for the causes, one thing I think is clear. It is not attributable to any pugnacious streak. The greyhound, unlike the bull terrier, tends to be comparatively timid of man and other animals. The turning of a head in a race is more likely to be an invitation to gambol than a serious attempt to savage a rival. The fact that there is no fighting on the coursing field where both dogs are utterly engrossed in their efforts to take their quarry, suggests that boredom behind the lure may be one of the basic factors.

All pure coursing strains had an inherent and primitive interest to chase live hares, but some strains were clearly less selective about what they chased. It was these strains, e.g. Mutton Cutlet, that handed on the genes that provided the most receptive actors for the new sport of greyhound racing. It soon became apparent that even among these track strains were individuals in which the chasing instinct was aroused by some particular type of equipment.

Some strains were more interested in the McGhee, McWhirter or Ball hares which are small and close to the ground and resemble the real thing. Others were less selective and were just as interested in the low flying type of object, the Sumner hare, which with its noisy trolley seemed to stimulate and retain the interest of a great number of greyhounds.

It is noteworthy that in the States, where the incidence of interference is probably lower than it is in the UK, the hare is driven much closer to the dogs than here. Almost under their noses. Moreover, two hares are not infrequently mounted on the arm, all of which intensifies and maintains their interest.

It is significant, however, that a relatively high proportion of interference takes place on those tracks where the hare is not stopped on or about the bend following the winning line. It is notorious that on tracks where the hare is taken away at full speed around a further two bends before the brake is applied, the tiring greyhounds tend to play with one another which in itself sows the seed of interference.

Whatever the cause, from the point of view of finding winners and certainly of avoiding losers the ability to assess a dog as 'awkward' before the Racing Manager has done so, or possibly before he has had the courage to act on his own impression, will certainly stand the assessor in good stead.

The enthusiast who is prepared really to study his subject will not be long in coming to the conclusion that if the race does not always go to the swift, or to the one that takes the shortest route home, or to the fastest starter, then there must clearly be some quality or compound of qualities that go to the make-up of a star greyhound. How otherwise can he explain those dogs that sometimes run up a dozen consecutive wins all in the highest class? How else can he explain the dogs that win two or even three classics, or those that win three or four of the prestigious Opens?

Versatility. Therein lies the clue to the really first-class greyhound and certainly to the great greyhound. To be able to win consistently on all shapes and sizes of tracks, on all conditions of going and from all traps, requires something more than mere speed or even the basic ability to 'run a curve'.

Clearly the consistent winners were not all trap 1 or trap 6 specialists, for at one time or another they occupied all six boxes. Just as certainly they were not always clear at the first bend. Nor for that matter did they always get tight on to the rails. Inevitably in some of their races they were baulked and bumped and did not get a clear run, *but they still managed to win*! The student eager to assess the capabilities of racing greyhounds would do well to learn to recognize the one quality common to nearly all the high-class trackers – versatility.

The student aspiring to greyhound racing 'know-how' may well inquire just what versatility amounts to in a tracker. Basically the answer is a dog's ability to place itself; to adapt its tactics according to the circumstances in each race; to pick its path through and round its converging rivals; instinctively to avoid coming on the inside or outside of a dog it senses is going to veer or waver.

Track craft and versatility are one and the same! The ability to avoid trouble – that is certainly the common attribute, the hallmark of most of the great trackers who have adorned the Hall of Fame. Certainly without track craft, without versatility, even the greatest trackers would have been ill equipped to handle the different types of hare and negotiate the infinite variety of contours and conditions of tracks throughout the country.

Variations, in fact, in the stage on which the artist must necessarily perform and which is the subject of consideration in our next chapter.

4

How to Assess
a Track

Just as there are horses for courses so too there are dogs for tracks, or should it be tracks for dogs? Just as there are some short tight little courses on which some horses can never do themselves justice, so too there is an even greater variety of greyhound racing tracks on which some dogs simply cannot give of their best, or vice versa.

Although all horse race-courses in England differ in shape and contour, the basic surface is always turf. Greyhound tracks on the other hand vary not only in shape and contour but their surface also varies from grass to sand, from sand to peat, and with various combinations of both, e.g. grass with sanded bends. It is therefore arguable that the physical aspects of the track have an even more important influence on a dog's performance and therefore on its chance of winning a particular race.

Most clearly, anyone aspiring to winner spotting in greyhound racing, must logically be prepared to apply himself diligently to a consideration of the physical conditions of the track on which his runners are expected to perform.

The type of dog that can negotiate a wide galloping track like Hackney or Shawfield is not likely to be at home on a shorter, tighter circuit like Derby. Similarly the type that can nip briskly round the bends at Catford where the premium is on agility and railing, is not likely to be as successful at Wolverhampton, where the premium is more on the ability to stretch out up the back straight.

The effect of the contour of a track on a dog's performance can best be illustrated by a study of the times registered by top-class greyhounds over the same distance but at different tracks.

As the hallmark of a great racing greyhound is his ability *consistently* to give of his best, the two stars, Pigalle Wonder and Mile Bush Pride (see Chapter 12), afford excellent illustrations of the effect of a track's contour on their performances:

	Best Time Wembley 525	Best Time White City 525
Pigalle Wonder	28·78	28·44
Mile Bush Pride	29·07	28·57

The practical and logical conclusion to be drawn from this comparison is that White City is approximately 0·40 seconds faster than Wembley, which in top-class racing terms amounts to about six lengths!

In terms of practical winner spotting, if Wembley staged an Inter Track race with White City with the latest times of the three White City dogs at White City clocked as 29·20, 29·30 and 29·40, and the times of the three Wembley dogs clocked as 29·30, 29·40 and 29·50, then the perceptive student bent on making his racing pay would be reasonable entitled to back the Wembley dogs on the score of the track variation factor.

To illustrate further the effect of contour on performance, one has but to note that Yellow Printer held the 525 yard record at the White City, 28·30, and also at Shelbourne Park, Dublin, 28·83. The logical conclusion is that Shelbourne Park is approximately 0·50 seconds slower than the White City. A factor which most astute English buyers take into account when looking for bargains for the Greyhound Derby! In this connection incidentally it is noteworthy that most Irish tracks are considerably slower than their counterparts in the United Kingdom in spite of the fact that on many of them only two bends are negotiated.

Where it is not possible to apply a common yardstick in the shape of the *same* dog's performances in gauging the 'pace' of two distinct tracks, the 'track record test' is generally indicative of the difficulty of a particular circuit. A glance at the following chart of track records, invariably held by top-class greyhounds, suggests that say, Brighton and Cardiff, are probably between 0·40 and 0·50 seconds slower than the White City.

Tracks like Hackney and Rochester which are also 1 second to 1½ seconds slower, illustrate the fact that yardage is not the most significant factor in assessing the characteristics of any track. Men may talk of one track being *faster* than another but from the dog's point of view it is simply more *difficult* to negotiate.

In this connection there can be no doubt that the degree of a track's difficulty is inherent in its shape or contour. Most tracks are ovals but there are ovals and ovals. To put it another way there are thin ovals and fat ovals! It is apparent from the following illustration that although the circumference of each may be identical, say 400 yards, any animal or human for that matter, racing thereon would find track A more difficult to negotiate at speed than track B (figure 2). A dog endeavouring to run the

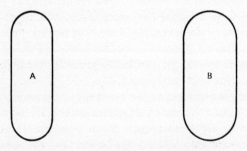

Figure 2

tight bends and curves on B would necessarily have to brake to slacken its pace otherwise the pull of centrifugal force on its thews and muscles would force it out on a wider course with a consequent time loss. The flatter or rounder the curve the more freely a dog can stretch out, as distinct from the short fox-terrier-like jog with which some greyhounds negotiate the tight bends of some tracks.

Another aspect of a track's shape which has a pronounced effect on a dog's ability to negotiate it is the degree of the banking on the terminal curves. One has but to consider the banking at such old time motor racing circuits as Brooklands to appreciate how it facilitates the negotiation of bends at high speeds. So too in a minor degree does track banking facilitate the dog's ability to run its curves.

Research is still being done into the cause and effect of the many injuries that beset the racing greyhound – the broken toes and nails, the pulled muscles, the track legs and chronic lameness. There are those advocates of loam, sanded bends etc. who believe that the answer lies in the texture of the track itself.

There are others, and I am inclined to subscribe to their view, who believe that the banking, or rather the absence of banking, lies at the root of the problem. Certainly when Shawfield (Glasgow) introduced banking on the bends for the first time in Great Britain in 1936 the reduction in cases of 'track leg' was dramatic. Of this at least I am sure, if the dogs themselves had to choose between well-banked tracks such as Glasgow (Shawfield), Harringay and Manchester (Belle Vue), and others less sympathetically constructed, like Walthamstow, I know which they would choose.

Such then are the geometric factors that the student seeking profit from his interest in the Dogs, will take into account, in addition to the relative merit or form of the runners themselves.

Before I leave the purely physical factors that must influence a greyhound's performance, there is one other geometric consideration to be taken into account. On large tracks like White City and Wembley which have a circumference of 498 and 463 yards respectively, it is possible to stage a standard 525 yard race with the minimum of overlapping, with the dogs being asked to negotiate four bends only. At smaller tracks it may be necessary to send the runners round, or partially round, another bend to complete the 525 yard trip.

As no animal can run a curve as fast as it can stretch out on the straight it follows that an extra bend necessarily slows down the overall time for the race, which probably accounts for the extreme divergence of times for standard distances on the track record chart.

Table 1 Track Record Chart

TRACK – British	525 yards Record (seconds)	Slower than White City (seconds)
Brighton	28·71	0·41
Bristol	29·24	0·94
Brough Park (Newcastle)	28·83	0·53
Cardiff	28·80	0·50
Hackney	29·30	1·00
Harringay	28·89	0·59
Leicester	28·85	0·55
Perry Bar	29·24	0·94
Rochester	29·97	1·67
Shawfield (Glasgow)	28·75	0·45
Sheffield	28·48	0·18
Southend	29·25	0·95
Walthamstow	28·95	0·65
Wembley	28·78	0·48
White City (London)	28·30	—
Wolverhampton	29·26	0·96
TRACK – Irish		
Celtic Park	28·86	0·56
Clonmel	29·40	1·10
Cork	29·10	0·80
Derry	29·56	1·26
Dandalk	29·32	1·02
Dungannon	29·18	0·88
Dunmore	28·90	0·60
Enniscorthy	29·50	1·20
Galway	29·54	1·24
Harolds Cross	29·03	0·73
Kilkenny	29·00	0·70
Lifford	29·40	1·10
Limerick	29·15	0·85

TRACK – *Irish (cont.)*	*525 yards Record (seconds)*	*Slower than White (seconds)*	*City*
Longford	29·32	1·02	
Mullinger	29·55	1·25	
Navan	29·17	0·87	
Newbridge	29·65	1·35	
Shelbourne Park	28·80	0·50	
Thurles	29·25	0·95	
Tralee	29·12	0·82	
Waterford	29·40	1·10	
Youghal	29·45	1·15	

But there are factors other than the geometrical ones of contour, banking and circumference which have a profound effect upon the speed with which dogs negotiate a track. I refer to the positioning of the starting boxes in relation to the first bend and the finishing line in relation to the last bend.

It will be apparent to all who take their greyhound racing seriously that the distance of the traps from the first bend must necessarily have an important bearing on the result of any race. On the assumption that more races are won or lost at the first bend than elsewhere it follows that the factors that may influence the dogs' positioning there are of paramount importance.

The greater the distance from the traps to the first bend, the better the opportunity for really fast trapping dogs with early pace to get round the first bend clear of their rivals. A glance at the table (see over) will indicate those tracks where the first bend is some 100 yards or more from the starting boxes and those where the distance is less than 80 yards.

The extra 30 yards affords the more talented dogs an opportunity of exploiting their superiority and of having a clear unimpeded run round the first bend.

If one should doubt the effect of trap location on a race one has but to consider the effect of moving the traps forward so that the run up to the first bend is reduced to, say, 30 or 40 yards. With

Table 2

Track	Yards	Track	Yards
Hackney	120	Southend	105
Wolverhampton	120	Oxford	105
Walthamstow	115	Willenhall	90
Bletchley	110	Hall Green	78
Crayford	110	Catford	75
Wimbledon	110	Perry Bar	70
Ramsgate	110	Brighton	66
Portsmouth	110		

such a limited opportunity to sort themselves out the inevitable result would be a first bend shambles.

There is just one other matter of equipment location which is important, although not to the same extent as the location of the starting boxes in relation to the first bend – the location of the finishing line in relation to the last bend. In those tracks where the winning post is almost right on top of the last bend then clearly there is little scope for the strong finisher to overtake the fading front runners. There is not a racing manager in the business who would deny that this sight – a strong finisher overtaking its rivals and getting up on the line – is the spectacle that really brings the crowd to their feet.

There is little to recommend the practice of backing strong finishers on small tracks where a short run from the last bend to the line puts a discount on the stronger finishing dog's ability to overtake.

But in addition there is another track factor which has an important influence on the performance of the tunners in any greyhound race – the state, or nature of the going. Unlike the Turf where the condition of the going on courses is traditionally described as 'Hard', 'Firm', 'Good', 'Soft' or 'Heavy' according to the amount of rain that has fallen, the going on greyhound racing tracks is not solely a matter of climatic conditions.

It is true that turf laid tracks are at the mercy of the elements just as race-courses are. Where the drainage is not completely effective it does sometimes result in heavy going or, as the Tracks term it, '0·90 seconds slow'. Where track maintenance in the shape of returfing is not carried out consistently, it is not unknown for the going on the rails and especially round the bends to be almost muddy and gluey. In circumstances such as these one does not have to be an intellectual giant to appreciate the advantage of backing not the railers but the dogs prone to middle track or even wide running!

But as I have indicated the going is not necessarily a matter of weather. Not all tracks in the United Kingdom race on grass: some race on peat, others on sand (waxed or otherwise), others on a combination of these. The figures in fact for the forty-two NGRC tracks are as follows:

> 25 on grass
> 9 on grass with sanded bends
> 6 on sand
> 2 on peat (Crayford and Gosforth)

In Ireland all tracks race on grass and at some the bends are sanded although not to any great extent.

That a track surface of springy well-drained turf is probably the ideal, few would care to dispute. The trouble of course is that it is difficult and expensive to maintain in perfect condition throughout the year. The disadvantage of hard frozen turf in severe wintry weather has to some extent been overcome by underground heating but even this has side effects. Certainly if under-soil heating is not carefully controlled it can result in soft treacherous going.

The fact that under-soil heating on a large scale is very expensive is probably the reason why several tracks in the United Kingdom still prefer to resort to peat during periods of frost. As for its effectiveness, much depends upon the state of the turf when it is applied and also the amount of peat necessary to provide an adequately protected running surface.

Not unnaturally a track so dressed feels so different from turf that it invariably has a distinct effect upon performance. Some greyhounds run relatively true to form on it while others show a distinct partiality or a complete aversion to the surface, which can have an effect upon the performances varying from 0·50 to 1·00 second, and even greater discrepancy allowances may be necessary where the surface becomes moist.

From the point of view of the student eager to pick winners there is one golden rule: during winter racing on peat the premium is on the dog that is going to be clear at the first bend and which is going to make every post a winning post. In front he is not going to suffer the inconvenience and discomfort of his rivals in the rear of having loose peat kicked up into his eyes or throat. A simple enough deduction? Maybe. But like most golden rules it is common sense.

Those tracks that favoured sanded bends were largely influenced by their desire to eliminate the many hock injuries that seemed to occur at the bends. Statistically they can claim some success, for with dogs getting their feet well into the looser surface their thews and muscles seem to have stood up better to the lesser strain and tension.

On the other hand there are those who claim that, although the sanded bend serves as a brake on a dog's speed and reduces the strain on bone and muscle, overall there are just as many injuries. This is because as soon as a dog strikes the turf coming out of the bend it acts like a springboard and puts all the stress and therefore injury proneness back again. Certainly the change in pace of the dogs as they move off the sand is most marked.

It is generally accepted that a *loose* sand/loam surface has little if anything to commend it. The punter finds it difficult enough to select his winners by a critical consideration of their relative pace and ability without taking into account the effect of sand half blinding and half choking the runners. If he has to choose, if he has to venture money in such conditions, there is only one dog to be on – the dog that he feels is going to make it all!

On the other hand it is not a far step from loose sand to well-rolled damp sand, and from damp sand to waxed sand, and from waxed sand to a mixture of well-rolled, well-raked loam and sand.

It is this surface which is adopted almost universally in the USA and which many racegoers on both sides of the Atlantic consider to be the perfect going for greyhound racing. Certainly it drains easily in wet weather and it can be watered simply and easily in hot weather.

Finally, and perhaps most important of all, the dogs like it, and for that matter so do the punters, for damp well-rolled sand and loam seems to provide a going that, taking one month with another, is probably more consistent than any other. Tradition and conservatism may well be too strong for sand/loam to supersede turf as a uniform going for greyhound racing, especially as not a few race-goers still believe that provided the bends are more generously banked, then grass is still the best racing surface in the world.

So much then for the contour, characteristics, size and surface of the tracks themselves, all of which play their part in influencing favourably or adversely the chances of a particular greyhound in a race. But what of the equipment most vitally involved in the chase – the hare itself? On the NGRC tracks the following types are installed:

McGee	17 tracks
Inside Sumner	15 tracks
Outside Sumner	9 tracks
McWhirter Sleigh	1 track

On the sixty-odd independent tracks it is noteworthy that no fewer than forty favour the inside Summer.

All have their own individual characteristics. The Summer hares for example run higher and in fact seem almost to fly like a skimming bird; they also have the distinct characteristic of a noisy trolley. The McGee hare on the other hand is smaller and runs closer to the ground.

This is no place to consider the mechanical merits of these different lures, but only to note that some dogs seem to chase one more enthusiastically than the other. No one knows just why. Only the dogs know and they have never told anyone.

On the other hand there can be no dispute that a change from an outside Summer to an inside Summer hare or vice versa, can and frequently does have a most marked effect upon a dog's trapping. Some of the most brilliant 'box hitters' become almost mediocre trappers when switched from a track with an outside hare to one with an inside hare. Just possibly they become accustomed to looking in one direction for first sight of the hare.

Whatever it is the effect is often most marked. Indeed, whenever there is an inter-track or open race at his local track, the racegoer bent on making his greyhound racing pay cannot afford to ignore the possible adverse effect of a change of hare on visiting dogs that on their home tracks were fast trappers and even close railers.

Unfortunately for punters, greyhounds are intelligent, affectionate, gregarious animals with a well-developed social sense, with a liking for the company of other greyhounds. They do not show their antipathy to a particular hare to the same extent as the famous Derby winner whose predilection for White City's was so strong that he would not even countenance the Wembley hare (at that time) and refused to chase it!

A very large proportion, uninterested in the lure, are nevertheless quite happy to gallop with the others all the way round a track without ever really chasing the hare in the sense of striving to reach it and destroy it. ('Chasers', in fact, as we dubbed them in the previous chapter.)

There is no faculty, no facet of critical judgement that a student of greyhound racing would do better to develop than this ability to distinguish between the dog that is really pursuing the hare with a desire to catch and destroy it, and the greyhound that is impelled by no such selfish zeal and is really doing nothing more than keep company with his fellows. The best clue to this vital information is just how a greyhound reacts and performs behind different types of lure.

Another physical factor which the student would do well to note is the effect on a dog's performance of first running under lights. Quite apart from those few tracks that stage afternoon meetings the greater part of racing in the summer evenings, with a last race schedule for 9.30 p.m., is conducted in natural light. As most newcomers – puppies and novices – arrive on the tracks in the summer months, say July, August or September, their first few months' experience in trials and races is therefore under daylight conditions.

The effect upon a sensitive highly-strung animal, first racing under lights, and emerging from the traps into a brilliantly lit circle engulfed in a black bowl of an arena, must be almost terrifying. Certainly the change is so fundamental that it would be extraordinary indeed if it did *not* have a pronounced effect upon its performance until at least it had learned to acclimatize itself to the new and strange conditions.

The message therefore that should come through to any perceptive student diligently searching for winners at odds that represent value for money, is to ignore entirely all young and novice greyhounds racing under lights, no matter how 'well' in they appear on the form book and time test, until they have turned in performances under lights comparable with their day-time record.

Observance of these rules, of using one's critical judgement to eliminate potential losers, is one of the great truths of greyhound racing. The surest clue to successful greyhound racing is to learn how to avoid losers rather than how to pick winners, for the simple reason that even on a selective approach there are so many more of the former!

5

How to Read
a Race

So much then for the power of the pieces and for the contour and characteristics of the board on which the game is presented, but what of the incidents, the various ploys of the pieces, which permit or prevent the pieces from giving of their best? I have previously stressed that if greyhound racing were conducted on a straight track of 400, 500, 600 or 700 yards it would not last a week as an entertaining spectacle, let alone as a betting medium – the same dog, the fastest dog, would win nine times out of ten. It is the bumping, baulking and manoeuvring for position at the bends that makes greyhound racing the exciting, thrilling sport it is.

Over a lifetime of greyhound racing I can fairly say that I have personally known many consistently successful punters. Men whose enjoyment over the years has not cost them a single penny, but who have had their fun and enjoyment for nothing. Men whose profits from greyhound racing have frequently subsidized the cost of their annual family holiday abroad. Taken individually it would be difficult to find any one common denominator. The four that I have in mind certainly come from very different walks of life.

There is Mr A for instance, a lecturer in pure mathematics at Oxbridge whose IQ would certainly be not less than 130. There is Mr B to whose skill and delicacy with the ophthalmic surgeon's scalpel not a few of his patients owe their sight. On the other hand, by academic standards neither Mr C nor Mr D can be regarded as intellectual giants – the former from his stall in the market dispenses some of the most succulent jellied eels I have ever tasted.

As for Mr D, a comparatively humble insurance clerk, thanks to his astuteness and success at greyhound racing, he is able to indulge such an excellent sartorial taste that even his directors must envy his appearance.

Superficially you would be right in saying that these four have little in common, but each of them – and all the others, too – have one common attribute, the ability to form a critical but dispassionate judgement of the events that occur during a greyhound race. They bear testimony to the basic truth that the key to transforming greyhound racing from an enjoyable entertainment into a profitable pastime is by the exercise of self-control, sound judgement and honest thinking.

To illustrate the point, just ask your friend after a race where No. 2 was at the second bend, what happened to No. 3 at the last bend and where No. 5 was at the pick up. In all probability he will say that he did not notice them because he was watching No. 1, the dog he had backed. What is more, he will probably add that he thought No. 1 was very unlucky because it was slowly away or crowded at the first bend, or forced wide at the last bend, etc. etc.

In short, he did not watch a greyhound race, he watched *one* greyhound racing. The one he backed! Worse still, he was prepared to look for all the bad luck that befell it (and to imagine some, too) merely to bolster his own hasty and ill-considered judgement.

Moreover, in all probability he will back the same dog next time out against some of the same dogs, oblivious of the fact that if he had watched carefully it would have been apparent that the really unlucky dog in the race was No. 4 who was carried out at the first, bumped at the second, and impeded at the last bend, yet still managed to finish close up third and was five lengths ahead of the field at the pick up!

Basically this is the Mr Folly of greyhound racing, the fan who can never hope to win consistently. It is commonly accepted by those who are most proficient in the art of race reading, that the first steps can best be learned by minimizing the task, by halving the field, and noting the progress of three of the six runners – say the first three round the first bend. One can then fill in the gaps and check up on the reading of the race by referring to the race card's account in the next meeting's programme.

By way of further simplification it is pertinent to add that although there may be, say, eight 'happenings' in a race it is unusual for more than a third to have an effective bearing on the final result of the race. Some for instance merely affect the runners in the rear who are not in contention anyway.

The whole purpose of race reading is quite simply to try and assess a dog's ability and the extent to which it is prevented from exploiting that ability by incidents in the race. There are those who would contend that this ability to observe and note all the movements of six dogs is a gift. This is not so. It is a faculty that like any other can be learned by dint of concentration on the task.

Furthermore it is seldom necessary to concentrate for the full 30 seconds of a race. It will certainly simplify the aspiring race reader's task if during the early process of learning the craft he concentrates on the following critical facets of the swiftly moving spectacle.

Focus Point One – *The Starting Trap*

It is as transparent as it is axiomatic that what happens here invariably has a material effect upon the result of any greyhound race – certainly those up to 525 yards. In fact, next to the first bend, it is probably the most influential point in any greyhound race.

One does not have to be an intellectual giant to realize that with a start like that illustrated in figure 3, the dog with the best chance at this stage of the race is No. 6 who broke fast and looks like having an unimpeded run to the first bend. No. 4's clear run looks like being nullified by arriving at the bend in the rear of 1 and 6 and possibly even behind 3. No. 2 is clearly going to be chopped between 1 and 3, who in turn look like bumping one another.

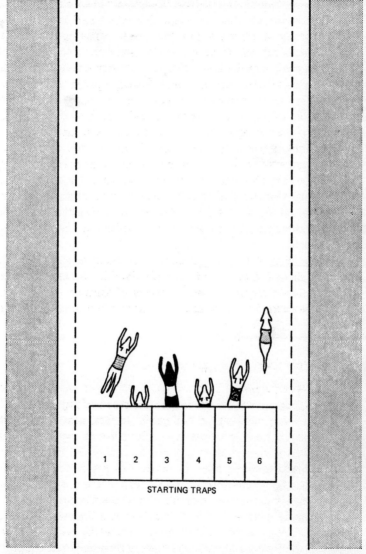

Figure 3

No. 5 on the other hand looks like being last at the first bend and on a wide outside at that.

The reader, now well versed in the assessment of the characteristics of the dog (Chapter 3) and the consequences that logically flow from these happenings, will avoid this type of race like the plague for it is a classic example of the punter's nightmare or conceivably the bookmaker's dream. The extent to which the permutations of such happenings would be multiplied in a race involving eight runners can best be left to the imagination.

Let us look at it again. A fast trapper in 1. A slow starter in 2. A fast trapping railer in 3. A slow starting middle track runner in 4. An average trapping wide runner in 5, and a fast trapping wide runner in 6. All the ingredients of a first bend shambles!

The only reasonable bet in such circumstances would be No. 6 and its chances are dependent upon its clearing No. 5 at the first bend, which may be difficult if the latter has good early pace. Even more significantly, the angle of 5's exit from the box suggests that it might well be bent on interfering with 6 – whose chances are accordingly minimized.

The first step in race reading starts with the mental mapping of the relative positions of the runners at the traps and then its transcription on to the race card.

Focus Point Two – *First time over the Winning Line*

Normally situated some 40 yards ahead of the traps, this is a good yardstick for judging the important quality of early pace. Although fast trappers frequently maintain their initial start and are also first over the winning line, this is not invariably the case. Some quite average trappers have a wonderful gift of electrifying acceleration, of getting into their top gear in a few strides and leading in the 40 yard dash to the line. Even more important, they often extend their lead at the place where it really matters – the first bend.

Following the race diagrammatized in Figure 3 one would normally expect No. 6 to cross the winning line ahead of the field

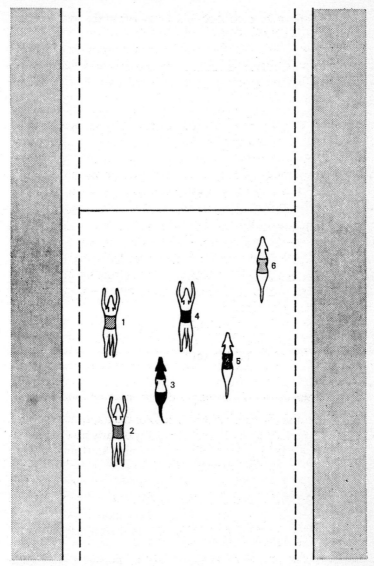

Figure 4

in view of his smart break from the box, but if No. 4 for instance leads him by virtue of his brilliant acceleration, then, having regard to the latter's relatively tardy break, he too must be noted carefully as the possessor of exceptionally smart early pace. But if 6 does not win this race he is certain to win others when graded fairly.

No aspirant to critical and therefore profitable race reading can afford to ignore the markings on his card which indicate those dogs on his track with this ability to jump off and be clear away. Some tracks openly acknowledge the importance of this faculty – first time over the line – by adding it to their race cards.

Focus Point Three – *The First Bend*

More races are won and lost here than at any other stage of the race. Even the most casual racegoer, the most superficial of fans, switches on his concentration at this stage of the race. It is understandable why this should be the most critical point. Six dogs – and in the States and Australia *eight* dogs – all travelling at their top pace have to brake and modulate it in order to negotiate the curve. At the same time inevitably dogs in traps 5 and 6 come in off the camber of the bend and converge towards the rails. This is where dogs can be squeezed on to the rails, chopped between two others, cannoned into, bumped, baulked, or simply sent flying head over heels. The first bend, that is where it can all happen.

Basically there are two opposing forces operative here. Dogs in traps 1 and 2 who have maintained their position in the run up, close to the rails, inevitably steady to adjust their balance and frequently move out a little from the rails to enable them to negotiate the curve more smoothly. The dogs in traps 5 and 6 on the other hand tend to come in with the camber of the track towards the rails. If 3 and 4 maintain their trap lines at the bend the possibility and indeed the likelihood of bumping and baulking is obvious.

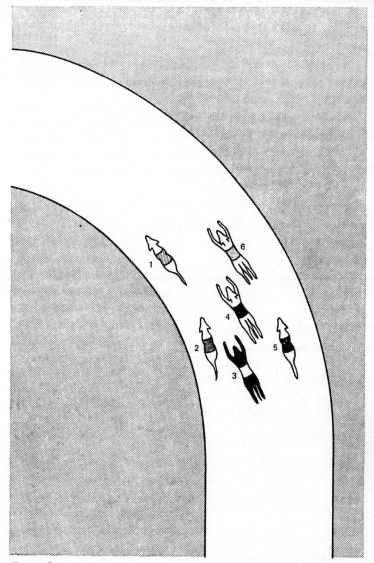

Figure 5

Continuing a study of the race on Figures 3 and 4, the fan aspiring to read figure 5 critically would make the following notes at this juncture:

No. 1 although coming off the rails has still had a clear un-impeded run thanks to smart trapping and taking the shortest route.

No. 2 by swinging out has bumped No. 3 and finally chopped it between 4, thereby putting itself and 3 virtually out of the race.

No. 4 although not physically bumping 5 has nevertheless carried it wide and made it check and change its stride. Although now in third place 4 looks destined for trouble at the next bend if 6 comes off the camber towards the rails.

No. 6 although having as trouble free a route as No. 1 has persisted in its wide outside and has lost ground by adding yards to its trip.

Although there is bumping and baulking at bends other than the first, the field is then invariably more strung out and the effect is therefore less eventful and decisive. As far as the second and fourth bends are concerned the dogs have come off the curve and are therefore not travelling at the same breakneck pace as at the first and third bends where they have the impetus of straight pace behind them.

Focus Point Four – *The Second Bend*

Unlike the first bend where the race reader's attention should be riveted to the position of the runners as they go *into* it, the note-worthy feature of the second bend is how the dogs come *out* of it and head for the back straight. The alert race reader should watch particularly how dogs impeded at the first bend are able to recover some of the leeway at this stage of the race.

A careful reading of the race at this stage would be as follows:

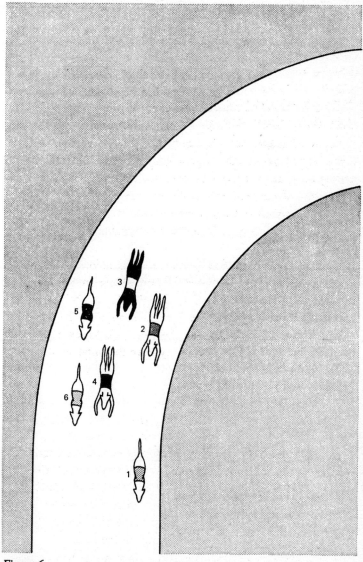

Figure 6

No. 1 has continued to lead and is making the most of its unimpeded 'solo'.

Nos. 2 and 3 have bumped each other out of contention by clumsy running.

No. 4 has cleverly avoided the trouble threatened by No. 6 coming over to the rails at the first bend and has in fact moved up to a challenging position.

No. 5 has simply wandered and run 'green' – is showing signs of a potential frustrated fighter.

No. 6 has continued its trouble-free course but still on an extravagant high wide and handsome route.

Focus Point Five – *The Back Straight to Third Bend*

It is along this 120 yard straight that the race reader looks for evidence of real pace as distinct from the ability and agility to run fast and well-balanced around curves.

It is noteworthy at this stage that:

No. 6 has exploited its superior pace to lead the field but again on the wide course that adds to its trip.

No. 4 has matched it stride for stride up the back straight and is clearly well in contention now.

No. 1 has had its limitations for pace exposed by Nos. 4 and 6 but its position on the rails will save it vital lengths in the run in.

Nos. 2, 3 and 5 are clearly no longer in contention as far as the placings in this race are concerned.

Although no experienced race reader would claim that the third bend is uneventful it does not normally have as critical an effect upon the result of a race as the other focus points. It is significant too that for the observer in the stands or at the winning line what happens at the third bend is the least visible of all!

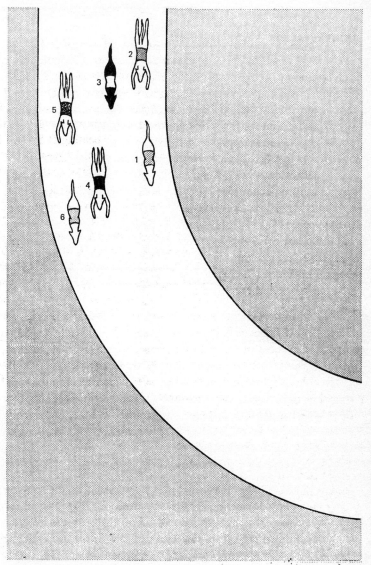

Figure 7

Focus Point Six – *The Last Bend*

As the place where the chips are really down, what happens here is clearly important. Just as on the Turf horses begin to 'fan out' for their home run as soon as they make the last bend so too do dogs at greyhound racing. There are those, and I am one of them, who consider that on the strength and evidence of what happens here a greyhound's character can be most clearly read. Not for nothing has the last bend been dubbed 'the moment of truth'.

It is here when the field enters the home straight that one can best identify the determined greyhound that is really putting it all in, who is wholeheartedly chasing the hare as distinct from those 'social' dogs who are only galloping with the others. As they round the last bend and head for the line this is when one can get a valuable line on the most important factor in a racing greyhound's make-up – its determination and genuineness.

In our particular race the reader will have noted that:

No. 1 by dint of clever tight running on the rails and taking the shortest route home has made up the leeway and overtaken both 6 and 4. The question now is whether it can hold on to its lead in the 50 yard dash to the line – will it stay the trip?

No. 4 still well placed to challenge. If No. 6 moves in to the rails there is danger of bumping. On the other hand, the tendency for dogs at the last bend is to move off the rails – will it stay the trip?

No. 6 ideally placed for exploiting its superior pace in the next 50 yards – will it stay the trip?

Nos. 2, 3 and 5 not in contention.

It is significant too that when dogs are tiring at the end of their trip latent interfering tendencies are most likely to manifest themselves. The race reader will be on the look out for the tiring dog that comes off its true line to 'lean' on the dog ahead. This is often the first indication of the potential interferer, and the race reader may turn such advance information into profitable

Figure 8

account when summing up a future race in which the potential delinquent is involved.

This race from the last bend to the winning line in addition to patently exposing the 'fader', the dog that does not stay the trip, is equally frank in its exposure of the 'chucker', the dog that in spite of coming into the home straight with a good lead patently begins to shorten its stride and falter as soon as it hears the drum of the pads of its rivals catching up on it.

Chicken-hearted dogs, like many humans and horses, can be brilliant performers as long as things are going their way, as long as they are winning, but simply have no stomach to battle on when the going is tough.

Focus Point Seven – *The Winning Line*

Although this is the pay-off point of any race, it is oddly enough the least important from a *race reading* point of view. Everyone in the stadium can tell you the position at this point, and moreover the track photos and the Press will constitute a permanent record. The race reader himself however might well complete his card with notes like this:

No. 4 ran a good race. Average trapper. Useful early pace. Has track sense. First-class pace along the back straight. Genuine – stays the trip.

No. 6 Fast trapper. Good early pace. Confirmed wide runner. Good pace along the straight. May fade in the last 40 yards of a 525 yard trip. N.B. Almost sure to be in trouble from traps 1, 2, 3 and 4.

No. 1 Very smart trapper. Takes rails from first bend. Average pace on straights. One pace type – genuine. May not stay 525 yards in class D race.

No. 2 Slow trapper. No early pace. Consistent railer. Genuine plodder.

No. 5 Novice – ran very green – no idea of what it was all about.

No. 3 Never in contention in race – very moderate. Out of its class in this race.

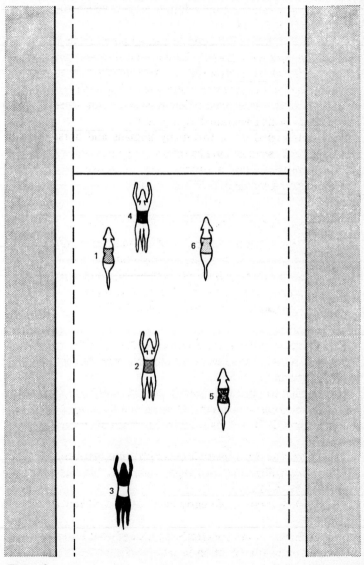

Figure 9

Focus Point Eight – *The Pick Up*

One of the most difficult lessons for the race reader to assimilate
is that although the race may be won when the dogs pass the
winning line, he cannot afford to switch off his concentration for
at least another five seconds. There may be a Race Result as soon
as the dogs cross the line, *but the dogs do not know it*. They are
still activated by their pursuit of the hare and as far as they are
concerned they are racing until the hare disappears or is thrown
off for them to pick up.

Although the majority of patrons will be making their way to
the bar – or to the bookmakers if they have been fortunate – the
dedicated student will continue to watch what happens in the
next 60 yards and note his card accordingly. If he does so in the
race that we have been following, his card might reasonably bear
the following further and important notes:

No. 4 continued to lead for a further 70 yards – clearly 600
yards will not be beyond him in future.

No. 6 after crossing the line was overtaken by 1 and 2. Clearly
at the end of its tether after 525 yards – not a staying proposition.

No. 1 has stayed on gamely – may well be even better over
700 yards. A sound genuine railer – just short of the pace required
to win a good-class 525 yard race.

No. 2 has been in trouble and in the rear of the field all the way,
but made up a lot of ground – some six lengths – from the line to
the pick up. Could well be much better than this race suggests –
finishes strongly – worthwhile supporting over 600 yards.

So much then for how to read a race and draw logical conclusions for future and profitable reference. But what of the
aspirant who is prompted to remark 'Yes, I know what to look
for and where to look, but *how* do I really go about it?'

Admittedly the ability to scan a field of six runners, mentally
noting what has happened to each and where it happened, does
not come overnight. It calls for concentration and in the early
stages not a little self-discipline. It would be as false as it is

Figure 10

misleading to suggest that a greyhound race can be transformed from a light-hearted form of entertainment into a consistently profitable pastime without some corresponding mental effort and application. But given this effort it is surprising how quickly he will assimilate the skills which are to equip him more than anything else for his tussles with the bookmakers or the Tote in his efforts to make his greyhound racing pay.

The ability to read a race is not primarily a matter of intellect – certainly not in the academic sense of the word. As I have indicated, there are too many people from differing walks of life, certainly of vastly differing IQs, who have excelled in their ability to read a race and draw sensible, logical and usually profitable conclusions from it, to associate race reading with intellect.

There is however one quality common to all astute race readers – the capacity for honest and dispassionate thought. They never, for instance, concentrate their attention on the dog they have backed, they allow their eyes and mind to flow along the line of runners, taking note of the sequence of happenings to the field in general.

Even more important, they never – repeat, never – make excuses for the defeat of their dog. They may note dispassionately but specifically that it was unlucky to be impeded at the second bend, but you are more likely to hear them express the view *when their dog*, say No. 6, has won, that the No. 3 dog was the unlucky dog in the race. The difference between excuses for losing and reasons for winning.

There in a nutshell is the psychological distinction between the race *watcher* and the race *reader*, between profitable and unprofitable greyhound racing!

The reading of a greyhound race and the attempt mentally to plot the positions of six runners at the eight focus points I have outlined is on a par with studying the moves in a game of chess. It can be done but to be effective, to be profitable, it must be done honestly and dispassionately. To do otherwise is simply to deceive oneself.

But having 'read' the race and having noted the important incidents affecting the result the question arises as to how best to record that information for future reference. It is expecting too much of the human mind to remember until the next meeting all the incidents in a single race, let alone in all the races, on a whole card. Some method of recording is necessary. Some of the most experienced and successful racegoers have found it convenient to adopt the official race card as the permanent record of their own race reading.

Incidentally the wealth of information that track managements furnish on their race cards never ceases to astonish horse racing fans. The name, breeding, sex, age, colour and weight of the animal together with the names of owner and trainer, the dates, details and times of its last four races or trials, its position at all four bends, as well as the distance by which it won or was beaten together with the actual time if a winner or its calculated time if beaten, all this appears on the official race card.

As if this were not enough, an official estimate of the condition of the going expressed in decimal points of a second is furnished, and, to complete the picture, the betting price at which it started.

Racegoers have become so used to this invaluable information service that they virtually take it for granted. They would do well to remember sometimes that in the sphere of the Turf the famous Time Form Service acquired a well-merited reputation for invaluable classified and expert information that is little more extensive than that incorporated as a matter of routine in most greyhound racing programmes.

But orderly and informative though it is, there is still scope for the race reader's own notes, for the record of what *he* saw happen and his conclusions therefrom. These notes can often be made most convincingly and legibly in the broad watercolour ink from the popular felt pens, which has the advantage of being 'see through'. Incidentally the most skilled race readers seem to make the fewest notes – their notes making up in perception and accuracy what they may lack in quantity.

The aspirant to race reading perspicacity will almost certainly find a need to resort to some readily understandable personal shorthand which may take some such form as the following:

FA   Fast away – trapped quickly
SA   Slowly away – trapped slowly
EP   Good early pace
B(1)   Baulked, bumped at first bend
B(2)   Baulked, bumped at second bend
W(1)   Ran wide at first bend
W(3)   Ran wide at third bend
P(2–3)   Fast along back straight
I(1)   Impeded at first bend
I(2)   Impeded at second bend
FF   Finished fast
NS   Did not stay – faded
Stg   Stays on

There will be scores of other informative abbreviations that commend themselves including the least complimentary NBG!

The margins of the card of a perceptive reader of the race we have diagrammatized may well bear the following notes:

No. 1   Rails – Stg
No. 2   SA – I(1) – B(2) – Stg
No. 3   FA – B(1) – outclassed
No. 4   SA – EP – P(2)(3) – FF – Stg
No. 5   SA – W(1)(2)
No. 6   FA – EP – W(1)(2)(3)(4) – P(2)(3) – NS

When next you see a fan at your local track thumbing through a wad of old race cards, carefully studying the notes he has made on previous occasions and obviously making a mental comparison of past results for assessment purposes, then in all probability you are watching a man who gets the maximum pleasure, and probably profit too, from his sport.

But the current recording on the race card of events as they happen does not fully meet the needs of those race readers who wish to be on a par with the Racing Manager in regard to cumulative and classified information. Those who are diligent enough have found it invaluable when they get home to transcribe the notes from their race cards on to some such easy reference chart as Table 3, a facsimile of the one that the Racing Manager himself has in his office.

The annotated race cards themselves form a record of what happens in each race in the programme, while the cumulative form chart serves as a summary of those cards and in particular as a record of the character of the dog and its style of running. From an easy to read chart such as this the race reader at a glance can see whether a dog is on the up-grade or down-grade, what is its best racing weight, when and in what conditions it recorded its best time, the trap from which it runs best, and by reference to its starting price whether or not it is a dog that runs best when it is 'wanted', etc.

Admittedly the compilation of such a form Chart will make demands upon the time of the race reader. It also makes demands upon the Racing Manager and his staff and if the race reader wishes to pit his wits against the Race Manager he must be prepared to make a similar degree of effort.

In point of fact once a foundation has been laid by extracting the official information from, say, the last six race cards, it does not take long to keep the chart up to date by transcribing the results and notes from each night's racing on to the chart. At the most say, half an hour, twice weekly.

From the systematic layout and easy-to-read nature of the form chart the intelligent race reader will be able to grade his dogs class A, B, C, etc., vital information that race cards in the UK – unlike the U S A – do not publish. Moreover it will be simple to review this classification in the light of, say, the dog's performances in each two month period. With his statistical proof of a dog's condition, whether it is 'up and coming' or 'down and going', together with the notes abstracted from his race cards, the race reader will be as well-briefed as the Racing Manager.

From this position of strength he is then, and only then, in a position to back his judgement. Not necessarily against the Racing Manager, for in many cases he will find that he is in agreement with his assessment, but against the Tote and the bookmakers.

Table 3 Chart Record for reference

	CLASS	Current Grading Figure	MEETINGS	1 Jan 1973	8 Jan	15 Jan	22 Jan	29 Jan	5 Feb	
ABBEY HILL (D) (April 1970)	B	29·50	Trap	1	3	4	3	2	2	
			Finish	1	4	4	2	2	1	
			Time	29·45	29·70	29·75	29·40	29·45	29·35	2
			Winning Time	29·45					29·35	
			Winning Weight	71½					71½	
			Betting Price	5-4	3-1	3-1	2-1	2-1	7-4	
BARNABY (D) (July 1971)	C	30·50	Trap							
			Finish							
			Time							
			Winning Time							
			Winning Weight							
			Betting Price							
CARRIE LEE (B) (March 1970) (*)	B	29·55	Trap	3	4	3				
			Finish	4	1	1				
			Time	29·55	29·40	29·10				
			Winning Time		29·40	29·10				
			Winning Weight		62½	62				
			Betting Price	4-1	5-2	6-4				
DARK PILOT (D) (June 1970)	A	29·30	Trap	2	2	3	3	4	6	
			Finish	1	1	3	2	4	5	
			Time	29·25	29·20	29·40	29·45	29·40	29·50	2
			Winning Time	29·25	29·20					
			Winning Weight	74½	74					
			Betting Price	3-1	5-2	3-1	9-2	9-2	3-1	
EVERGLADE (B) (February 1968)	D	29·85	Trap			4	4	3	2	
			Finish			3	3	2	2	
			Time			29·90	29·85	29·50	29·45	2
			Winning Time							
			Winning Weight							
			Betting Price			3-1	7-2	7-2	3-1	

13 Feb	26 Feb	5 Mar	12 Mar	19 Mar	26 Mar	2 April	9 April	16 April	23 April	30 April	NOTES
		4 5 29·70 5-1	4 3 29·60 4-1	1 2 29·35 7-4	1 2 29·30 6-4	2 4 29·70 4-1	5 4 29·80 4-1	5 6 29·85 3-1	3 2 29·40 9-4	2 1 29·35 29·35 71½ 6-4	Fast trapper – Tight railer Trap (1) Trap (2) 'Specialist' Most effective when money is down – an 'off when it's on' dog!
		4 5 30·90 8-1	6 6 30·95 8-1	6 5 30·80 7-1	5 3 30·40 5-1		3 2 30·60 3-1	2 2 30·60 7-2	2 1 30·50 30·50 69½ 3-1	2 1 30·40 30·40 70 5-2	Big soft puppy – very green – 19 months old. Had rough trip first three outings Just beginning to get the idea of racing. Runs better from inside traps Has potential – sure to continue to improve – sure to attain class B
							4 (T)3 29·85	2 (T)2 29·75	2 29·70 8-1	1 3 29·65 5-1	Came into season 16 Jan '73. *Watch about 18th week, 14 May to 21 May* First Trial 9 April '73 Fast trapper – brilliant early foot Tight railer – consistent – determined – won five races in row last season Litter sister won classic 'Laurels' *Sure to 'spring' in May*
30 1	6 4 29·40 5-2	1 1 29·30 29·30 73½ 5-2	1 1 29·25 29·25 73½ 9-4	2 1 29·15 29·15 73¼ 2-1	3 29·30 9-4	1 3 3-1	4 3 29·35 3-1	5 3 7-2	3 1 29·20 29·20 72¾ 2-1	2 1 29·15 29·15 72½ 7-4	A 'cracker' – best dog on the track – wins small opens Hits the box – fast up to first bend Clever runner – avoids trouble – consistent Still overweight – running better as racing weight falls Invariably first at 'pick up' Almost certainly stays beyond 525 Note to watch for first outing over 600–650 yards
45 2	2 1 29·80 29·80 71½ 5-2	3 2 29·55 9-4	3 3 29·80 3-1	6 2 29·50 7-2	6 DNF 4-1		6 DNF 3-1			4 2 29·57 5-2	Tender footed veteran – must have soft going Clumsy runner – knocked over twice – DNF Been on injured list. Getting past it? Blatant chaser – races for company – has run 2nd in 29·45 – class B time! Last won trouble-fraught race

6

How to Analyse
a Race

So much then for reading the incidents of a race. Consider now the constituents of a race and the factors actually involved in its make-up. Just as the regular reader of a newspaper soon acquires a facility in solving its daily crossword puzzle simply because he has learnt how the puzzler's mind works, so too can the race-goer obtain invaluable clues to the solution of the problems set in a race by trying to discover the aims and objects of the person who compiled the problem – the Racing Manager; in short, by getting into the mind of the person who set it.

Those disgruntled punters who sometimes complain that the Racing Manager has just thrown a race together, are merely exposing their own lack of intelligence. No Racing Manager who habitually put fast trapping wide runners in trap 1 and fast trapping railers in trap 6, who merely attempted to befuddle patrons by 'shuffling the pieces' so that luck was the determining factor, would last a month in the highly-organized entertainment business that greyhound racing has become.

The student of greyhound racing would be well advised to proceed on the assumption that when a Racing Manager puts a certain dog into a particular trap, or for that matter in a particular race, he has some very good reason for so doing. It is the race-goer's job to try and ascertain just what those reasons are. By analysing the make-up of a race he will be on the way to assessing more accurately the relative chances of the dogs and thereby be one step nearer to foreseeing the result of the race.

Broadly speaking, the primary aim of most Racing Managers is to compile and present races that will prove interesting, varied and exciting to the track's patrons. The most successful managers in fact will often admit to grading some races more closely than others, and even to compiling a proportion of races in which some dogs have better chances than others according to the merit of their past performances.

At least one of the most respected Racing Managers in the business admits that he does not aim at compiling races that will puzzle everyone and result in the broad betting of 7-2 the field, but rather to grading at least some of the races on the basis of a reward for effort, i.e. to grade some races that will give intelligent racegoers an opportunity of doing a little better than the foolish gambling ones.

Bearing this in mind it clearly behoves the student to discover those greyhounds which the Racing Manager considers possess better chances than the others. In other words, to identify those runners that might qualify as a 'good thing' from the punter's point of view.

Before attempting to crack their professional secrets, to discover the clue to some of the problems they set, let us see how the average Racing Manager sets about his duties.

To begin with he has his own form chart – probably covering all of one wall of his office – of all the dogs with the track's trainers, be they resident or dispersed. From these a certain proportion must be eliminated – those on the injured list, bitches in season, newcomers that have not yet completed their trials and dogs that have conflicting Open Race engagements. The net result is a list of available greyhounds, or to use the official term – the track's racing strength.

Against all of these greyhounds will be a continuous running record, not only of their recorded times over the track's various race distances but also the information that appears in the official race cards, i.e. weights, traps, age, etc. From a glance at the most recent times, say their last six races, he can arrive at a factor that can best be termed the 'current grading figure' for each greyhound.

It is inevitable that the only individually recorded times are those of the actual winners of races or trials. The times of the other runners must necessarily be calculated times. Broadly these are arrived at by adding to the winner's actual recorded time 0·06 of a second for each length between the winner and the other members of the field. If for instance dog A wins its race in 29·50, beating B by two lengths and C by four lengths, then the calculated times of B and C for the purposes of the record chart and subsequently the official race cards, will be 29·62 and 29·74 respectively.

Just as the dog's current grading figure does not mirror the *slowest* time recently recorded, equally so it does not necessarily reflect the *fastest* time recently recorded. If there is one thing on which most Racing Managers agree it is the wisdom of treating with caution fast times recorded by winners in a lower grade of race. Experience has taught them that these winners are frequently incapable of reproducing these fast times in grades of comparable class.

The lesson for the punter is obvious. When next he sees a dog that had previously won in a poor class race (say the second race on a card) in runaway style in 29·50 and it is raised in class to the fourth race in which the fastest time of the runners is 29·90, then this is anything but the good thing that the figures appear to purport. Whereas the dog had pace enough to trap clear and virtually have a solo against less talented opponents, in this higher class it is most unlikely that it will get a clear unimpeded run.

As the current grading figure attributed to each greyhound is based on and reflects the merit of its recent times, it represents the time that a dog can be *expected* to record in its race. If it does not do so, then critical race reading should identify and diagnose the reasons and causes why it did not do so. On such 'post mortems', on such incisive race reading, are future profits made. Most certainly the Racing Manager's form chart next day will record his diagnosis of the circumstances.

With a current grading figure allotted to each dog on the

racing strength, the Racing Manager now has the basic material on which to prepare and compile his card of eight six-dog races for the forthcoming meeting. In addition he has to grade a reserve for each of the eight races and probably two for the Quinella races. Fundamentally his aim is the selection of some sixty greyhounds capable of division into eight groups or races, so equally matched that no members of any groups will prove too markedly and therefore embarrassingly superior or inferior to its fellows with which it has been grouped.

But important as the time factor is in the grading of greyhounds it is only one of the factors affecting its selection in a race with five other rivals. To quote an extreme case, if the sixty dogs selected in six groups of eight for the night's programme were all slow trapping wide runners, or were all fast trapping railers, then the night's racing would be a chaotic shambles – a bookmaker's fiesta!

Clearly the Racing Manager has to take into account, the dog's style of running – those dogs that are consistently fast or slow trappers, those that rail or take a wide course, those that have early pace or finish strongly, and of course those dogs with several permutations of these qualities. His task therefore is to correlate these styles of running, together with their current grade figures, in such a way as to ensure his public a reasonably trouble-free race and one in which all have a chance to give of their best.

More than one Racing Manager has assured me that once he has sorted out his candidates for a race on current grade figure lines, if he were free to do so, he would then compile his race on some such lines as the following.

Table 4 Possible race make-up

1	2	3	4	5	6
Fast starter	Slow starter	Fast starter	Slow starter	Fast starter	Slow starter
Railer	Railer	Railer	Middle tracker	Wide runner	Wide runner
Fader					Strong finisher

One has but to ponder the latent plan behind this set-up to appreciate the commendable object of the Racing Manager – a trouble-free race in which each greyhound has full scope to exploit and display its pace and cleverness without interference.

Unfortunately he is not free so to do, for the rules prescribe that for all graded races trap positions shall be governed by a draw, with the proviso however that where there are one or two dogs which are accepted as wide runners then they may, at his discretion, be allotted to the outside traps 5 and 6, with a view no doubt to eliminating or reducing the risk of a trouble-fraught race.

While on the subject of traps it may well be timely at this stage to consider the effect, if any, that a dog's trap position has upon the race. I appreciate that there are scores of regular fans who night after night and week after week back certain traps at their local track, say trap 1 or trap 6, throughout the whole race programme, regardless of the calibre of the dog therein.

There are even those who carry this unthinking routine one degree further and for example back two traps consistently in a Forecast – say 1 and 3 in every race.

If they enjoy this simple little ploy then by all means let them do it, but if they merely want to 'play the numbers' and are too lazy even to try to exercise some judgement then why not play roulette or bingo!

To those who prefer to pick their winners by reference to trap numbers as distinct from the more critical and rational tests of form, fitness and family that will be outlined in the next chapters, the following may be of interest.

A statistical review of 8000 graded races over a five-year period at tracks as dissimilar in character as White City and Harringay, indicated that the winners came from the various traps in the following ratio:

Trap	Percentage
1	19
2	16·6

Trap	Percentage
3	15·3
4	14·9
5	16·7
6	17·3

Admittedly a marginal preference for traps 1 and 6, but one so minimal that no punter would be likely to grow fat on it.

The following statistics in relation to the prestigious Classics bear out the same conclusion that blind following of traps is not the key to profitable greyhound racing.

Table 5 Numbers of winners from each trap

Trap	Gold Collar winners	The Laurels winners
1	6	7
2	2	6
3	5	4
4	7	10
5	9	8
6	8	5
TOTAL	37	40

So much for the common view that Traps 4 and 5 are the handicap boxes! Clearly it all depends upon the type of dog occupying them.

This much then seems certain. Such an approach to greyhound racing – a blind unthinking allegiance to particular traps – is hardly likely to commend itself to the serious-minded student dedicated to the task of winner finding.

On the other hand it would be just as foolish to claim that a dog's trap was never a material factor in the result of a race. The nub of the issue – the importance or otherwise of a dog's trap – depends entirely on the calibre, characteristics and style of running, of the dog itself.

For instance it seems natural to conclude that the dog occupying trap 1 (or those in both 1 and 2) has an obvious advantage because it is nearest to the rail and therefore best placed for the shortest route home. But what if the dog in trap 1 is a slow starter? It may well be running close to the rail but this will be of little advantage with the backsides of three or four dogs obstructing its passage round the first bend.

What too if No. 1 does happen to be a fast starter but is also the type that without being a wide runner nevertheless moves off the rails at the first bend? In all probability if either 2 or 3 are railers, they are going to bump it out of contention when it swings out. In such circumstances, occupied by a dog with such a running style, trap 1 or 2 would be the very reverse of an advantage.

Traps 3 and 4 are often spoken of as the 'handicap boxes', presumably because the dogs there have two or more dogs on either side of them and have therefore twice as much chance of being impeded as the dogs in traps 1 and 6. But what if the dog in one of these traps is a consistent 'box hitter', the type that in the vernacular is 'off and away before the lid goes up'? Conceivably it will be off and away from trouble two lengths ahead of its more numerically favoured neighbours on either side. All the more so if in addition it has the gift of quick acceleration.

In such circumstances, occupied by a dog with such a running style, trap 3 or 4 would be no disadvantage.

What then of the outside trap 6 (or 5) to which the Racing Manager in compiling graded races has the discretion of allotting accepted wide runners? That the allotment of an outside trap favourable to its wide style of running is of itself no bonus is borne out by the fact that its occupant is virtually committed to a longer trip. This may be as much as 533 yards on a 525 yard track.

Even the argument that the dog in trap 6 is favoured because it catches the first sight of the hare, is invalid. As in the other instances quoted above the benefit depends upon the dog. Conceivably catching an early first sight, if it involves bouncing and bumping itself prematurely before the lid goes up, could well be a disadvantage. In any case not all tracks have outside hares!

I would be the last to claim that the trap draw had no significance. Most clearly it has. But as it is fortuitous and therefore beyond the control of the racegoer, it is clearly not in the same category as those physical factors considered in Chapter 4.

But of this I am certain. Those who have made their greyhound racing most pleasant and profitable have invariably given infinitely more thought and consideration to the character and capabilities of the dogs that happen to occupy the traps than they did to the allocation of the traps themselves.

But in addition to a dog's current grading figures and its style of running, there are other factors which the Racing Manager will take into account when compiling his race cards. He will, for instance, have regard to a dog's time and performance in relation to its weight. If it is running faster as its weight reduces, or vice versa, it may well be that it is running itself fit – into tip-top condition, and that the next variation, even of a quarter of a pound, may really put it on its toes. When a dog really begins to 'spring' it is not unusual for it to make its current grading figure look rather silly.

Nor will the Racing Manager ignore the age and experience of a dog. A puppy learning its game is unlikely to appreciate and give of its best in a 'rough and tumble' race. On the other hand, should such a novice puppy be clear at the first bend and have a clear run throughout, it may well register a time that makes the Racing Manager's face red with embarrassment.

To come to such a conclusion just one race earlier than the Racing Manager – therein lies the challenge and certainly the reward of the astute racegoer. As the reverse of the coin, the young puppy may equally well 'duck' the issue through sheer inexperience at the first bend and finish tailed off. As a result he could conceivably be dropped in class for his next race and with a better run round the first bend the outcome might well be entirely reversed.

But it would be an undue simplification of his responsible job to suggest that even such factors as weight and age are the boundaries of the Racing Manager's consideration. Such psychological factors as the effect of having been knocked over, or badly chopped, in a dog's last race, or of racing under lights for the first time, must be taken into consideration by the Racing Manager anxious to present greyhound racing of an even and therefore exciting pattern.

In his effort to get into the Racing Manager's mind, to understand the nature of the problems he is setting racegoers when he compiles a race card, the alert racegoer will soon discover that he has some advantages denied the Racing Manager. Broadly the advantage of being able to *particularize* as distinct from *generalize*. By the very nature of his job the Racing Manager has little choice but to generalize. The racegoer on the other hand is free to exercise his specific judgement and assessment.

By way of illustration, the Racing Manager may estimate the general going on a certain night to be, say, 0·20 seconds slow. When next day his staff enter up the details of the night's racing on his kennel charts – from which his current grading figures derive – marking up how each dog ran, where it finished, its weight, its winning or calculated times, then the latter will reflect the Racing Manager's general assessment of the going as 0·20 seconds slow for *all the dogs* that ran that night.

The racegoer on the other hand may have noted that on the inside 'lane', say up to 4 feet from the rail, where the turf is more worn and sparse, the going was much stickier and muddier. Moreover, it got progressively worse as the meeting progressed. In such circumstances the racegoer might come to the conclusion that the going for the railers was probably as much as 0·40 seconds slow. Conceivably for the wider runner on the good turf the going might well have been 'normal'.

The practical consequences of the racegoer's ability to apply his particular assessment to the Racing Manager's general assessment, are obvious. As the times of all the dogs that raced that night are adjusted by the going factor 0·20 seconds slow, the student has but to apply his personal calculation to the times of those dogs that he felt were not influenced by the condition of the going to the general extent of 0·20 seconds slow. As a result of his specific amendments, perhaps greater allowances for the railers and diminished allowances for the wide runners,

the racegoer may find that his adjusted times differ from those of
the Racing Manager's as follows.

Table 6 Adjusted winning times

Race No.		Trap	Winning or Calculated Time	Going Slow* Fast	Official Adjusted Time	'Specific' Adjusted Time
2	Belle	1	30·40	0·20*	30·20	30·00
3	Jet	2	30·00	0·20*	29·80	29·60
6	Avis	5	29·75	0·20*	29·55	29·75
8	Rio	6	29·60	0·20*	29·40	29·60

The practical application of this adjustment will bear fruit
when next these dogs race. The Racing Manager will have put
Belle in a race on the basis of a time of 30·20 whereas in the
racegoer's opinion that time ought to be 30·00. Logically therefore
Belle is in a race with up to three lengths in hand – a factor which
may or may not make it a good thing but at least one that improves
its chances and must clearly be taken into account when weighing
up the race.

Similarly when next Rio races it will be grouped with five others
on the basis of its time of 29·40. As the racegoer considers that
29·60 was a more realistic assessment of its time, then clearly its
chances are not enhanced, although not necessarily wrecked.

For the student anxious to probe the Racing Manager's mind,
to ascertain the factors he took into account when setting his race
puzzle, it is equally important to realize that in addition to the
individual assessment of the dogs on the racing strength he is
also committed to a broader group classification of those dogs.

To avoid the necessity of running down the names of all the
dogs on his form chart, of comparing the current grading figures
and times of some 200 greyhounds, most Racing Managers
necessarily rationalize their duties by arranging the list into several
groups, grades or classes, with the object of bringing together
for easy comparison those dogs of equal merit and ability.

The first step in any such system of classification is normally to fix the upper and lower limits. With these points determined it becomes a simple mathematical exercise to allocate the balance into as many intermediate bands as one requires. Conventionally many Racing Managers take as the top rung of their grading ladder the current grading figures of the track's best dogs, and as the lowest rung of their ladder the time band of its puppies and novice dogs, say those capable of 30·00 to 30·25 seconds for 525 yards.

Others adopt an alphabetical classification of the kennel's racing strength with Grade A reserved for the best dogs, Grade E for the most moderate dogs, and with the rest of the kennel's racing strength allocated in between those two on some such lines as the following:

Grade	Dogs within time band
A	29·25 to 29·45
B	29·45 to 29·60
C	29·60 to 29·80
D	29·80 to 30·00
E	30·00 to 30·30

If the track record was, say, 28·75, the Racing Manager might consider it helpful to have another super grade (virtually Open race Class AA) for dogs capable of beating 29·25. Similarly if the standard adopted for novice greyhounds and puppies is, say, 30·75 then there is logic in his adoption of an additional Duffer or Maiden class M for novice dogs 30·30 to 30·75.

There are few sayings more commonly heard on a race track than 'So-and-so is racing out of his class tonight' or 'So-and-so has been dropped in class'. An understanding of how the Racing Manager determines the grade of a particular dog will go a long way to enable the student to decide the significance of the comment – if any. More important still, it may enable him to decide whether it has any practical and profitable consequence!

The student can best critically assess the Racing Manager's classification of a dog by compiling his own register of the grade to which he considers it appropriate. Admittedly this involves further homework, but in greyhound racing, as in life generally, one only gets out what one puts into it. The Racing Manager and his staff to earn their salaries have had to work hard to compile races for the public's entertainment. It is a corollary that the punter must make a commensurate effort if he is to reap his own rewards.

This much is certain, few aspects of greyhound racing reward effort and study as richly as the analysis of the Racing Manager's race compilation. The top and bottom grades seldom present difficulties to the Racing Manager – nor opportunities for the punter. In the colour spectrum the determination of the bands of black and white present no problem; it is the sorting out of the various shades of grey that is supremely difficult.

Similarly in greyhound racing there are a great many dogs that do not fit neatly into the official grades. It is among these in-determinates that some of the best things from the punter's point of view are to be found. Classification is often a matter of degree, even of opinion, and here the perceptive punter and the Racing Manager meet on equal footing. The Racing Manager may give a dog the benefit of the doubt and put him in a Grade C race. The student in his evaluation of the dog's grade – see Chapter 10 – may decide that he is really a Grade B dog. Consequently as a dog running below its true class, if all the other factors are favourable – distance, trap, going, etc. – then a bet thereon would be justified, not dictated by frivolous fancy, but by deliberate consideration, by dispassionate reason.

Such indeed is the distinction between gambling and betting.

7

How to pick Winners: on Form

That it is possible to go greyhound racing for the first time and pick one, two or even three winners on nothing more than mere fancy or a fickle whim, is beyond dispute. Maybe just because red is a favourite colour, or four is a lucky number, or because that little black bitch looks 'lovely and cute'. Life is often like that – fortune not only favours the brave but also the foolish. For a short time. The difficulty is to transform the occasional fanciful winner, admittedly often at long odds, into a series of consistent winners that overall show a profit on one's operations.

Anyone who has borne with me so far will appreciate that the only way to succeed in making greyhound racing interesting, entertaining, and profitable, is to become an expert at your local track – become as expert as the Racing Manager. Clearly no one except a full-time racegoer can become an expert at three or four tracks. Life and time is too short to permit the necessary homework. The daily newspapers are the first to recognize this by appointing separate experts at the various London tracks.

Incidentally this may be a suitable opportunity to stress that a great many people lose the real enjoyment of greyhound racing simply because they are too anxious to win. The people who derive the greatest pleasure, and certainly the greatest profit, from the sport are those who exercise the most self-control, sound judgement and honest thinking. These are the qualities of the successful punter, whether it be on the Turf or on the greyhound track.

Perhaps the very first lesson to be learned in greyhound racing is that it is simply impossible to bet on eight races and consistently show a profit. When one has gone to the trouble of grading a race oneself, of analysing critically the factors that influenced the Racing Manager in compiling the race, it should become clear that at least three races on the card are so closely graded that they are simply not viable propositions. Not infrequently these unsoluble races involve the lowest and the top class dogs, the first and last races.

If the racegoer is honest enough to accept the fact that he cannot solve the puzzle then it is a clear sign that he appreciates both the difficulties that have confronted the Racing Manager and moreover the skill with which he overcame or even bypassed them in compiling the race. In such circumstances he should give the Racing Manager best.

In each of another two races a dog may stand out as being 'well in' but if these promise to be trouble-fraught races, then clearly they are not betting propositions. Of the remaining three races the critical racegoer who has done his homework may come to the conclusion that in Race 4 dog A has an outstanding chance, in Race 5 dog B has a better than average chance, and in Race 7 dog C looks almost a grader's 'good thing'. But even then it does not necessarily follow that these three dogs should be backed. The question of value for money (as we shall see in Chapter 9) comes into the picture even when one has deduced from a study of form the dog that ought to win the race.

But let us put first things first. The identification of the dog which has a better chance of winning than his rivals is the most significant factor in the operation of all winner finding. Consequently one must bear in mind that there are three separate and distinct aspects on which the racegoer must be reasonably well briefed before he is entitled to put his money at hazard on their probable performances.

First and foremost, he must have a sound knowledge of the calibre, characteristics and capabilities of the greyhounds that comprise the card (see Chapter 3). Secondly, he must have taken into account the effect of the contour and conditions of the track on which dogs will be expected to perform (see Chapter 4). Lastly, but by no means least, he must have analysed by reference to his comprehensive charts, the up-to-date form of each greyhound in the race (see Chapter 6).

Fortified with this basic knowledge, the result of careful homework, he is now in a position to apply it in practice. By way of a practical example I suggest we follow the movements of the model young racegoer, Mr Al Wise, who has diligently annotated his race cards and moreover kept his form charts up-to-date as recommended in earlier chapters.

He knows from experience that it is hopeless to leave his basic review for the bar or restaurant at the track. For one thing, he will not have the opportunity of easy reference to his form chart. For another, no sooner will he sit down than his pals, Tom, Dick and Harry, will descend upon him with such conventional inanities as 'I have heard so-and-so is off tonight', 'So-and-so will skate it in the fourth race', and so on. He has heard it all before so he pins his faith to the old adage 'Let your eyes be your guide and your money the last thing you part with.' Experience has taught him that his form chart is the best record of what his eyes saw, and that its study can only be done effectively *at home*.

A glance at the morning papers confirms that the first race is timed for 7.45. If he leaves home about seven o'clock he can get to the track about 7.15. As he had spent an interesting hour the night before when the runners appeared in the evening papers, he needs no more than half an hour to check the stadium's list of weights with his form chart.

He has decided to disregard the first race – for novice greyhounds and puppies. It comprises three newcomers with only trials and two public races to date. The others are old, tender-footed 'has-beens' from other tracks who, when they feel in the mood or are sure they are not going to be knocked about, occasionally give a flash of their old ability which would be more than good enough to win this race. But clearly they are no longer consistent or genuine enough to warrant a reliable form analysis to be drawn.

He now scans the runners of the second race with particular

reference to the current grading figures on his chart. Yes, this is clearly a Grade D race, with a time band of 29·80 to 30·00. He runs down the field comparing it with his form chart markings. Now let us see:

Trap 1 – *Apple Blossom*

Yes, his current grading figure is 29·80. Grade D. The notes column indicates that he hits the box quickly but comes off the rails at the first. A middle track runner. Clever enough to miss trouble. Appears to be running at his best weight 71½ lb. Finishes well. Consistent.

Trap 2 – *Florida Peach*

Current grading figure 29·89. Moderate starter. Little early pace. Finishes strong. Grade C before she came into season 14 weeks ago. Has had four races since returning to racing strength but has shown no indication of pre-season form. Down graded to Grade D.

Trap 3 – *Heavy Cavalry*

Current grading figure 29·90. Grade D. Heavy dog, 78 lb. Long strider – shows pace up back straight. Clumsy runner on the bends. Five years old – not likely to improve.

Trap 4 – *Forest Flash*

Current grading figure 29·94. Grade D. Smart trapper. Good early pace. Has been lame – must have soft going. Almost certainly a chaser – 2nd 30·48; 2nd 30·26; 3rd short head 29·64; 2nd 30·19.

Trap 5 – *Hard Tack*

Current grading figure 29·91. Grade D. Slow trapper. Very wide runner. Hit the box and was first last time out, in fast time, but in Grade E class – virtually a solo. Sure to be backed next time out. Fades and does not get the trip here.

Trap 6 – Heather Hero

Current grading figure 29·92. Grade D. Fastest trapper in race but slow to get into top gear. Middle track runner. Consistently improving puppy – has found two lengths each time out. Lacks experience – seldom misses trouble. Full brother to Eric the Red, big Open race winner. Sure to improve but may find the trip here a little beyond him at present.

What conclusions, what deductions, are to be drawn from this wealth of factual information thrown up by reference to his form card and racing charts? Let us follow our young friend's thought sequence as he ponders his problems.

First and foremost, it looks as though it should be a reasonably clean-run race. There are no such trouble-fraught factors as fast trapping, wide runners in traps 1 and 2 and no early pace railers in 5 and 6, or for that matter any 'nutters' in 3 and 4. On the face of it the element of hazard and chance seems to be minimal.

Good – now for the sort out. Florida Peach can surely be eliminated from the reckoning. She is barely fourteen weeks out of season, her weight indicates that she is a good 2 lb. above her best winning time and that she is still showing signs of maternal softness. It may be as well to make a note on her chart to look out for her about three weeks hence when she will be about seventeen weeks out and ready to 'pop' at any time.

Logically enough, A1 Wise rules out No. 5, Hard Tack, as a serious contender. True he was second last time out but he hit the box brilliantly which was totally out of character for such a consistently slow trapper. Moreover the very fast time that he recorded was in a low grade race and must therefore be suspect. On the other hand this fast time may well ensure a lot of money for him – the bookmakers might even make him favourite.

Nor can he go along with No. 4, Forest Flash, a confirmed 'chaser'. True, he could be first to the bend, but trap 4 will not help him here. Even if he does lead he is certain to let others take over in the back straight which will encourage him to fall in behind. The hot sun and drying wind these past few weeks will have made the going firm and this will not suit his tender toes.

Al Wise scans the card again. His preliminary analysis has left three live candidates, 1, 3 and 6. Of these, both 1 and 6 are faster trappers than 3 and have useful early pace. On all form it looks as if 1 and 6 will be clear round the first bend. The only danger here is Forest Flash, but the handicap-box, trap 4, should take care of him. Down the back straight it ought to be 1, 6, 4 and 3 in that order, with 4 moving up to the leaders at the third bend.

No. 4 will have 6 on his outside, 'leaning' on him and keeping him nicely placed about 3 feet off the rails. If No. 1 comes off the last bend first, or even level with 6, his superior finishing speed should certainly see him through. The only remaining question is whether the 'chaser' No. 4 has waited too long to catch No. 6 to run him out of second place.

On all logical analyses of current form Al Wise cannot resist the conclusion that everything indicates that No. 1 has a much better chance of winning this race than his rivals. The next mental step is to summarize his chances and those of the other runners in mathematical order, in much the same way as if he himself were making a 'book'. Taking all the factors into account Mr Wise arrives at the 'book' he would make of their chances something like this:

5-2	No. 1	Apple Blossom
3-1	No. 6	Heather Hero
3-1	No. 4	Forest Flash
7-2	No. 5	Hard Tack
7-2	No. 2	Florida Peach
5-1	No. 3	Heavy Cavalry

With his card marked accordingly he is ready for the next step in the process of making his greyhound racing pay – backing his opinion and pitting his judgement against the bookmakers – but only if he is assured of value for money. For him this is no vague theoretical phrase. He has already calculated what he considers to be value for money in this race and he will not bet unless he gets his considered odds or something better.

The next ten minutes of scrutinizing the market, the technique of the betting operation, is so separate and distinct from the process of winner finding that a separate chapter has been devoted to it.

Now consider Mr Wise as he is carefully scrutinizing the runners in the third race.

A quick reference to his current grading figures confirms that this is a Grade D race, with 4 and 5 ex-Grade C dogs who are on the way down. As he runs through the race card comparing the notes he has made during his hour of homework he shakes his head 'I see he has put Flying Fox in Trap 6 again. The fastest trapper in the race and sure to come over to the rails at the first bend. Those other two early pace "quickies" 3 and 4 look like being chopped and no mistake.'

He sees from his notes that No. 2, also a smart trapper and originally a tight railer behind the inside hare at his previous track, tends to move very much off the rails here to the outside hare. On the face of it the race seems made for No. 1 who looks assured of a clear run all the way round. Unfortunately he really does not get the trip here and fades badly. Whatever comes out of the second bend within five yards of him – and it could be any of three dogs – is certain to catch him.

No – this is no betting race. It certainly does not seem up to the Racing Manager's usual high standard of compilation. Maybe he left it to the assistant Racing Manager, maybe he just had an 'off' day – after all even Homer nods! But as far as our friend is concerned he has no qualms about his determination to sit this race out.

The next race however is clearly a different kettle of fish, for a similar analysis suggests that the consistent Black Prince should have a lot in hand of his rivals here. The Press seems to think so too for he is freely napped by several correspondents. If the bookmakers will allow him to bet, Al Wise is prepared to back his judgement, but only at his assessment of the risks involved – certainly at odds of not less than 2-1.

Focus Point 1. A perfect break, staggered enough to avoid impeding at the box. Priority at the first bend now depends on early pace.

Focus Point 1. A bad start. Number 2 hopelessly 'chopped', numbers 1 and 3 on a collision course, number 6 stumbling and unbalanced, numbers 4 and 5 look set to go clear.

Focus Point 2. First time over the line. Superior early pace now asserting itself.

Focus Point 3. The first bend, the 'clear' reward of fast trapping and early pace.

Focus Point 4. The back straight – the long stretch where the premium is on pace, pure and simple.

Focus Point 5. The last bend – dogs fanning out for clear run. Tiring dogs beginning to fade.

Two frames showing a greyhound at speed and illustrating the perfect stride length

When he turns to the fifth race a run down the current grading figures tells him that this is a much better class race, Grade C with some of the runners on the up grade. Good – the better the class the more consistently they run. His form chart notes indicate:

Trap 1 – Rebel Chief

Current grading figure 30·09. Average trapper. Moderate early pace. Tight railer. One pace type that gets the trip well. Small whippety dog – has been off the track for some weeks. Promising trial times suggest the rest has done him good. Has been favourite when he has won most of his races. An off when it's on dog!

Trap 2 – Scarlet Cloak

Current grading figure 30·15. Smart trapping bitch. Good early pace. Clever runner – very fast up back straight. Was Grade B before resting. Won two small Opens before coming into season. Has been disappointing since return. Has led to last bend in last two races then faded unplaced.

Trap 3 – The Hussar

Current grading figure 30·20. Slow trapper – sometimes misses break completely. A one pace 'plugger' – no early pace. Approaching veteran class. Begins to run at 525 mark – might be useful over 700 yards. A bit of a 'mud lark'. Completely genuine.

Trap 4 – Hot Pants

Current grading figure 30·18. Fair trapper, shows good early pace from box 1 or 6. Does not relish jostling at traps or bumping at bends. Has shirked the issue in last two races – either very nervous or chicken-hearted, probably the latter as his sire was a 'soft' front runner.

Trap 5 – More Haste

Current grading figure 30·22. Slow trapper. Middle track runner. First race for two months. Solo trial times suggest he is not back to old form. Racing Manager has not been very kind –

he should be in a lower class than this. Sound and completely reliable. Certain to be the big outsider on the books.

Trap 6 – Wedding Present
Current grading figure 30·18. Average trapper – very wide runner. Clumsy – does not get the trip here. Has been on sick list with shoulder trouble more than once.

So much then for the specific race card notes and the form chart's overall appraisal of the talents and traits of the runners. Now let us listen to Al Wise thinking aloud again.

'It looks as though the Racing Manager has designed this as a patent three-dog race – 3, 5 and 6 have no real chance on form, not in a true-run race anyway. There should not be any first bend trouble.' Having eliminated this trio, he now pursues his reflections. 'I cannot see 4 getting clear at the bend when she has dogs on either side of her – anyway I'm sure she is a "chucker". That leaves 1 and 2.'

He thumbs back on his cards and notes the date that the bitch in trap 2 was last in season, takes out his diary, turns to the calendar and for a moment is lost in count. 'Hell's teeth, she is seventeen weeks out now and she has not "popped" yet. Those two last races when she led most of the way were probably the first signs of her really "coming on". It has got to be No. 2, but if there is any money for No. 1 it might be prudent to have a "saver" or even a forecast on the Tote.'

Having made his considered selection he casts his mind back over the chances of the other dogs and comes to the conclusion that odds of less than 2-1 against Scarlet Cloak would underrate the chances of Rebel Chief and Hot Pants in particular.

With his mind made up on this question of value for money our friend makes his way down from the stand towards the bookmakers for the next phase in making his greyhound racing pay. We shall meet him very shortly, after he has applied two more tests to his selection's chances of winning the race in question – the tests of Fitness and Family.

8

How to pick Winners:
on Fitness

That form is of paramount importance in the selection of winners brooks no dispute, but the student would be ill-advised to regard it as *all*-important. *Very* important – yes. The *most* important factor – probably yes. But the only factor worthy of consideration – a thousand times no. But some of the aspects that have already been written into the form chart – the dog's weight variation, its age, its propensity for lameness, etc., are not strictly form factors but rather physical factors which of themselves are worthy of separate study and consideration. The most important of these recognizable by inspection is physical fitness.

A dog at the very peak of its physical condition, trained to the minute as the Press often has it, will certainly run a better race than one that has not yet reached that peak, or one that passed that peak some weeks ago and is now both physically and mentally stale. There are few trainers who would not subscribe to the view that many a dog becomes mentally stale before it becomes physically stale.

The importance of having selected a dog that is really sharp and fit can be judged by the fact that most races are won by dogs that find little more than three lengths – 0·18 of a second. If you wonder whether the difference between being just fit and really rarin' to go can cause such a disparity, just ask any experienced trainer. The answer is likely to be as illuminating as it is confirmatory.

As for those who would argue that fitness can be judged from a study of a well-kept form chart – to the extent that a dog's most frequent winning weight is the best measure of its fitness – this may well be true as far as it goes. Unfortunately it just does not go far enough!

As it is clearly impossible to handle the runners, the physical fitness of a greyhound can only be appraised by inspection, by visual examination, when it is on parade. Just as I am always impressed when I see a student thumbing through a wad of old race cards, so too am I equally impressed when I see him walking down from the stands to get a close-up of the dogs either in the paddock or track parade. Certainly it is but common sense to seek the support of one's eyes for the conclusions drawn from a critical study of form.

It would be foolhardy to deny that some of the oldest of sporting sayings seem to deny the test of physical perfection, for example, that greyhounds (like horses) go in all shapes and sizes, or that a good greyhound (like a good horse) cannot be a bad colour. Certainly there are countless examples of ugly ducklings who gained classic successes – Wild Woolley with his Staffordshire bull terrier aspect, Beach Comber ('Shorty') come readily to mind. Other examples too can be cited to support the view that when it comes to racing talent it is very often a case of 'handsome is as handsome does'.

But for all that, there are those, and I am one of them, who still adhere to the conviction that those ugly ducklings would have been even better and faster if their conformation had more faithfully complied with the standards of physical perfection set out in Dame Julian Berner's *Boke of St Albans* written as long ago as 1481:

> Headed like a snake
> Neckt like a drake
> Backt like a beam
> Sided like a bream
> Tayled like a rat
> And footed like a cat

It may be true that they go in all shapes and sizes but there is one rule that I have found to be invariably true – all the *very* fast dogs are *very* good-looking. By that I mean that they do not have any outstanding vagaries of conformation. Such stars as Future Cutlet and Mile Bush Pride come most readily to mind.

But what does the perceptive fan look for as he watches the paddock parade? He has done his homework, studied his race cards and charts, and has reduced the field to three or probably four runners. He has taken initial stock of the early betting market and is now looking for some further evidence in the shape of physical factors that may influence his choice one way or the other or conceivably persuade him not to have a bet at all.

Broadly he is *looking* for those indications of physical well-being that his hands could have told him for certain by *feeling*. At the Sales he could have run his hands over a dog's loins to feel the pliant firmness of a really good back – the hallmark of a fit animal. He would also have felt the width between the shoulders and the 'set on' of the blades. For it is skeletal factors like these that govern the length of stride of any racing animal.

Moreover he would certainly inspect the vital digits, toes and nails, for 'big' or 'knocked up' toes or for that matter missing nails and digits with particular reference to any which had been removed.

But although he cannot apply the *sensual* test of his hands there are plenty other physical signs that he knows are indicative of a dog's ability, or especially its inability, to gallop smoothly. He may observe obvious faults in conformation, which are inconsistent with the generation of racing speed. Floppy soft splay feet, knock knees and tucked in elbows are invariably the signs of poor rearing and a dog which has been badly reared cannot possibly run really fast. It is, incidentally, during the rearing period from two months to twelve months that more greyhounds are ruined than at any other stage in their lives.

On the parade too one can easily spot cow hocks – that mal-formation that is a virtual embargo on racing pace.

There is also the appearance of the dog's coat, not its colour which is of no significance whatever, but its condition. There is nothing so clearly indicative of good health as a sleek glistening coat. A glossy silky sheen is the hallmark of a dog that is on its toes and ready to go. For one thing it tells not only of external cleanliness and good gloving but also of inner health.

There is an old saying that 'when the coat dries up form dries up'. Certainly one would be wise speedily to eliminate from final selections any dog with a harsh staring coat. Just indeed as one should ignore any dog that was clearly coating. The moult both in the animal and bird world is an enervating and weakening process that invariably saps physical fitness.

The racegoer seeking the evidence of his eyes will look favourably, too, on the well-balanced animal – the big heavyweight dog that somehow does not *look* big and heavy. He will look askance at the dog that carries a physical virtue to excess, for example, a long back that is just a little too long in proportion to the length of its legs.

The age-old Turf saying 'A good walker is invariably a good galloper' will afford him yet another visual test to apply to his form selections. A greyhound of pace, like a horse so endowed, invariably walks with a liberty of action that is as obvious and pleasing to the eye as it is indefinable. The free and confident stretching out of the forelegs, the crispness of the steps, these are facets of a style of walking which is stamped with a certain exhilaration and grace which tell of lithe and supple muscles in a well-trained animal.

In short, the observer's eyes – an intelligent scrutiny of a dog's style of walk on parade – will tell him what an expert's hands would so easily ascertain, the condition of the propulsive muscles on which a greyhound's speed depends. On the strength of this study he will be prepared very quickly to revise his views of a dog which appeared, when halted before the stands, to be in the pink of condition with its haunch and thigh muscles simply bulging, but which, when led around, broke into a slow laborious walk more reminiscent of a muscle-bound shot putter. Such a one often gallops like a cart-horse in slow motion!

The way a dog carries his tail is also an invariable indication of its physical fitness. No one expects to see a greyhound carrying its tail high like a happy beagle, but on the other hand it is anything but a healthy sign if it hangs down straight, limp and loose. Tail carriage in fact can be one of the most reliable barometers of tip-top racing fitness.

The tail in any animal is an extension of the spinal vertebrae. The most important muscles in a greyhound's conformation are those along the dorsal and loin areas, those that lie along each side of the backbone. Unlike the racehorse which when galloping puts its hind legs on the spot its forelegs left, the greyhound puts its hind legs a good distance ahead of the prints of its forelegs when in full gallop. To achieve this he must necessarily bend his back to a considerably greater degree than the horse. His backbone in short is virtually a spring operated by the dorsal muscles, which explains why they are the most important in a greyhound's physical equipment.

If these dorsal and loin muscles are in really good shape – like firm pliant rubber – then that firmness will extend down to the caudal muscles for the tail is an extension of the spine. As a result the base of the tail of a really fit dog will often jut out a little and not lie flat on the buttocks.

There is yet another aspect of a dog's behaviour and appearance pattern that (for those with eyes to see) is all revealing. The hallmark of a greyhound in really tip-top condition can often be gauged by its inability to stand still. Even when its handler halts it seems to be eager to bounce like an animated indiarubber ball. Not tugging madly at the lead but just moving incessantly from one foot to the other while its head is turning attentively in all directions.

There is no more encouraging sign than to see one's form selection with its coat bright and gleaming, physically bouncing, kicking up the ground when it stales and showing every sign of mental alertness. Such a dog is really fit and well and in a condition to give of its best. This, together with a favourable form calculation, may well be good enough to win the race.

When the calculating racegoer arrives at the track and has his list of the weights of each runner, he can make yet another physical test. He can compare the racing weight of his selections with their best running weight as extracted from his form charts and transcribed on to his racing card. A dog may have only varied 1 lb since its last outing – well within the stipulated 2 lb limit – but it may still be 2 lb above, or below for that matter, the weight at which it has won most of its races, i.e. its best winning weight. This may well be the factor which influences the critical racegoer to disregard him as a probable winner of this particular race.

But above all there is one other physical factor which is so important that our friend has starred and made a special note of it on his form charts at home – the seasonal dates of the bitches on the night's programme. There are surely few racegoers, who have not at some time or other backed the track's best bitch, usually a local favourite on its return from seasonal rest, largely on the strength of its excellent performances before it was rested. In its races in the thirteenth, fourteen, fifteenth and sixteenth weeks it is hardly ever in contention and often brings up the rear.

On such form the Racing Manager has no alternative but to drop it in class, but to no avail. By about the seventeenth or eighteenth week, when most of its fans have written her off in disgust either as a 'goner' or a rogue, then suddenly in its next race it flashes out of the traps, makes every post a winning post, and wins by ten lengths in one of the fastest times of the night. To add insult to injury, as befits a bitch that has let its supporters down for the past five or six weeks, it probably starts as an outsider at remunerative odds!

The Joe Follys in the crowd invariably 'blow their top' when the bitch has found 0·70 seconds – the game is crooked – the trainer and owner have 'had it off' – the Racing Manager should be lynched – the stewards should hold an inquiry – and so on. In short, in their frustration they blame everyone except themselves for a disappointment that arose only from their own ignorance or carelessness.

The physiological aspect of a bitch's heat or oestrum are simple enough. Most bitches come into season twice a year and are then prepared to be served by a dog. Once mated, the whole process of motherhood slowly unwinds in its natural course and during the nine weeks of gestation the bitch tends to build up both natural fat and a milk supply for her puppies. What is not so generally known is that these same natural physical phenomena also occur in a bitch – to a lesser degree – that has not been mated and is therefore not 'expecting'. There is the same build up of natural fat and creation of maternal milk, a condition clearly inimical to the physical fitness of a racing greyhound.

It is for this reason that the NGRC rules prohibit a bitch from racing until twelve weeks after its coming out of season. But even when it does return and has had its grading trials it is often but a shadow of its former self. For race after race it is never more than briefly in contention, recording times probably not within 0·75 seconds – twelve lengths – of its old grading figure.

If dogs behaved like this after a lay-off for injury then in all probability the fans would regard him either as unsound or jaded, but for bitches invariably more genuine, game and consistent than their brothers, a perfectly understandable solution is available in the shape of Mother Nature.

The perceptive racegoer, seeking to make his greyhound racing both pleasurable and profitable, recognizes this female pheno- menon, this tendency for a bitch to have a sudden revival, really to 'spring' some time after the sixteenth week from coming out of season. He has therefore marked that week and the succeeding week on his form chart with red crosses to ensure that he does not overlook it. If the bitch does not 'pop' in those weeks, he will follow it consistently because he knows that Mother Nature never fails.

Over and above all the many other indications of physical well-being that he has learnt, from the glossy coat, the bright eye, the alert head, the strong jut of the tail and the crisp step, he has come to rely upon the indefinable jaunty sexiness of the female whose ovaries are generally reminding her that she feels good and looks good!

As he strolls away from the paddock satisfied that Scarlet Cloak's physical condition more than confirms its Form chances, our friend leans on the rails and for a few moments gives his mind to a consideration of breeding – the Family test.

9

How to pick Winners:
on Family

From the point of view of finding winners it would be misleading to ascribe to a dog's pedigree anything like the same significance as its record of performances, its form. Nor is it as important as those physical factors that advertise its fitness. Yet it would be equally misleading to dismiss it as of no significance whatever. Those who get the most enjoyment (and if enjoyment and profit are not synonymous at least in a betting sport they are near allied) out of greyhound racing are those who appreciate that greyhounds are not machines. They are lovely, lively animals, and they are flesh and blood each with its own parents and grandparents and further ancestors.

Every greyhound on a race card, therefore, has inherited in some degree or other the talents and traits, the calibre and character, of one or more of those ancestors. Some may have inherited the ability to hit the box like rockets, others to sustain their brilliant pace over longer distances than the others. Some may inherit mental characteristics of a less desirable nature – a tendency to interfere or a duck-hearted reluctance to contest the issue once it is headed in a race.

Some certainly inherit purely physical factors like coat colour or even quality of bone that makes them more prone to break hocks and toes than other strains. That the extent of this hereditary transmission in the sphere of greyhound racing is nothing like as clear-cut as on the Turf is unfortunately true. To that extent it remains both a reflection on and a challenge to greyhound breeders. But more of that anon.

The drawback to pedigree as a practical aid to winner finding lies in the fact that racing ability, sprinting and stamina, are not simple attributes like coat colour. Each is a combined attribute embracing a number of factors, skeletal, myological, nervous, vascular, respiratory, of which every one is controlled by its own particular gene pair. When a breeder tries to evolve a dog that will gallop faster between two points than the others, he is up against the difficulties of multifactorial inheritance involving the capacity of the heart, lungs, circulation, soundness of limb, correct conformation giving activity, nervous energy allied to temperament, and the greatest imponderable of them all – the will to win (see Chapter 12).

Small wonder then that most successful racegoers long since made up their minds that the family's place in any winner finding operation is complementary and subordinate to the other factors of form and fitness. They know that every mating presents an astronomical number of possibilities in the offspring, and that all that the most dedicated student of pedigree can do begins and ends with an attempt to envisage the more *probable* of those manifold possibilities.

Logically therefore the pedigree element must necessarily be subordinate to the factors of form and fitness. Blood alone is no guarantee of ability, but it can and often does enable the student to make up his mind between two animals which on form and fitness appear to be inseparable. Pedigree, in short, is merely something to study for background, not for backing!

On the other hand it would be an extremely foolish man who would seek to reject the breeding details on a race card as so much irrelevant rubbish. To do so would put him on a par with those who consider that greyhound racing is nothing more than a game of animal roulette featuring trap numbers, coloured jackets and electrically recorded times.

Let us suppose therefore that by way of extreme example the following problem is put to those who scoff at family and hereditary influence and who regard it as of less than no importance. Let us suppose that Mr Punter attends a local athletic meeting. The 100 yard invitation race has attracted an entry of four 18-year-olds. He has no information whatever of their previous form, no knowledge of the times they have done or the events they have previously contested. He is advised by one of the stewards however that runner A is the son of a British heavyweight boxing champion, B the son of a European weight lifter, C the son of a cross channel swimmer and D the son of an Olympic 100 metres runner.

To stabilize the other hereditary influence, the tail female, let us suppose that all four are sons of four sisters who played table tennis for England! In such circumstances, in the absence of form, which would Mr Punter back to win if he had to make a choice? The answer that the force of logic, reason and common sense evokes is surely the son of the Olympic sprint champion. How much more logical would his choice have been if he had also known that the mother of D was not a table tennis champion but was herself a British sprint champion and record holder.

This may well be an extreme example of the breeding factor but sufficient to rebut the fallacy that pedigree is of no account in the diverse and complex problem of winner finding at greyhound racing.

The Turf however illustrates the importance of pedigree even more patently. Let us assume that a five furlongs sprint at Ascot has attracted six maidens at starting, and each has run into third place in one or other of its last two outings in races of similar class. Two of the runners are by Grey Sovereign, two by Ribot and the remaining two by Chamoissaire. In the absence of any lead from their identical form or from the betting market, to which pair would an intelligent punter look for the prospective winner? Almost without exception most knowledgeable racegoers would certainly choose the pair by Grey Sovereign. Why? For the simple reason that the stock of Grey Sovereign is renowned not only for their sprinting speed over five to six furlongs but also because they mature precociously quickly. The distinctive feature of Ribot's stock on the other hand is their supremacy over ten to fourteen furlongs, while Chamoissaire's stock are invariably stayers who not only require a distance of ground to give of their best but also three or four years to come to hand.

Why then, one may ask, in addition to the clues of form and fitness, does family and breeding figure so practically in winner finding on the Turf? The answer shortly is that for the past 300 years horses have been carefully and selectively bred for the special purposes for which they were required. As a result of specialized breeding, strains and families have been evolved the members of which can be expected fairly consistently to conform to the pattern of their family.

One has but to scan the breeding of the winners of the great sprints of the Turf, the King's Stand, the Nunthorpe, the Cork & Orrery, the Diadem Stakes and the July Cup, to find the names of such sires as Sir Cosmo, Panorama, Gold Bridge, Whistler, Fair Trial, Court Marshal, Tudor Minstrel, Abernant and Grey Sovereign appearing with almost monotonous regularity.

At the other extreme if one runs through the winners of some of the great stayer's events, the Ascot, Goodwood, Doncaster Cups and Jockey Club Stakes, then such sires as Hurry On, Son in Law, Gainsborough, Trimdon, Precipitation and Alycidon, manifest themselves time and time again.

Even in the sphere of the Turf's great middle distance races the names of Blandford, Hyperion, Nearco, Djebel and Ribot, also occur in frequent repetition. So much so that the history of the classics in the past fifty years could almost be written around such names.

In this connection it is noteworthy that one does not find a sire of sprinters also figuring prominently in the stayers' list or vice versa. Nor for that matter is there much, if any, overlapping at either ends of the middle distance band. The degree of specialization has become so efficient and effective that it is now indeed eminently sensible for racegoers to rule out entirely a certain horse 'because he will never get the trip' or because the race is 'two furlongs short of his trip'.

It still remains true of course that animals are not machines and it is therefore unwise to dogmatize on the subject. But at least the specialization of the Turf breeder has ensured that the pedigree of his animals is a factor to be seriously weighed in common with form and fitness, and moreover the odds are heavily stacked against surprises.

One has but to scan the scrolls of greyhound racing fame to appreciate just how different is the scene. If one studies the winners of its prestigious sprint races, the Thames Silver Salver, the Scurry Gold Cup and the National Sprint, the sires whose names occur most frequently in the past decade are Hi There and his sons Crazy Parachute and Prairie Flash, in much the same way as do the sons of Grey Sovereign in the Turf sprints.

But if one similarly reviews the breeding of such stayer's classics as the St Leger, the Gold Cup, the Key and The Stayer's Plaque, it is as noteworthy as it is remarkable that the same sires Hi There, Prairie Flash and Crazy Parachute equally dominate the scene although the distance races are almost twice as great. In terms of the Turf this is the equivalent of Sir Cosmo or Grey Sovereign coming out as the most prepotent sire of winners of the Ascot, Goodwood or Alexandra Stakes.

Yet further testimony to the proof that breeding should only be considered as a background to backing in greyhound racing and not as a factor in itself, is borne out by the Turf's specialization in the National Hunt sphere, i.e. hurdling and steeplechasing. As most 'jumpers' are gelded, breeders aspiring to produce hurdlers and steeplechasers must necessarily look outside the ranks of those who have distinguished themselves over the fences. It is a tribute to their critical intelligence that over the years they have invariably discovered horses with the ability to transmit the jumping qualities they so keenly sought.

In the past thirty years such horses as My Prince, Cottage, Vulgan and Straight Deal stood out as the stallions to use if one wanted to breed top hurdlers or steeplechasers.

Hurdling in greyhound racing, on the other hand, has been with us now for close on forty-five years with its Grand National,

Wimbledon Gold Cup and Empire Stadium Hurdles, among others. But what attempt has there been to single out those dogs to which one could reasonably send a bitch if one wanted to breed hurdlers? In this connection greyhound racing breeders have not got the excuse of their Turf counterparts that hurdling winners are gelded!

But if the breeding details on the greyhound racing card are not of the same significance to the would-be winner spotter as they are to the racing man, I would stress once again that he would still be ill-advised to ignore them. At the very least they may well provide the final extra test to enable him to decide between two greyhounds which otherwise appear equal.

Oddly enough where the *family* influence is of greatest and most practical significance in greyhound racing is in the area where it is most neglected – the tail female. A successful prepotent stud dog may well have 50 to 100 bitches or more each year. Consequently he may well be represented by an annual crop of some 150 to 250 puppies, only a very small proportion of which will reflect his own talent. Such a small proportion that it would be difficult for even the most receptive memory to keep them in mind until they had established themselves by some memorable performances.

A truly prepotent bitch on the other hand is unlikely to have more than four litters in her lifetime and may be represented by little more than 20 puppies over a five-year span. But once she has produced a litter that 'hits the headlines' by virtue of their talent and successes it is more than a distinct probability that her other litters will be similarly endowed.

There are many – and I am one of them – who, when in doubt about a final selection in a race, would have no hesitation in going for the son or daughter of a proven winner-producing dam. Unfortunately breeding is a subject that too often gets lost in theory. It may be as well, therefore, to end on the following practical note. If a punter has to choose between two dogs equal on form and fitness and one is by an anonymous nonentity and the other by some well-known and highly successful sire, say Crazy

Parachute, Printer's Prince or Newdown Heather, then there are good practical reasons why he should go for the latter.

In the first place no sensible man is going to pay £100 for a stud dog's services unless he has reason to believe that his own bitch is worth that expenditure. In this connection she would only be worth such a mate if either she had been a good winner herself, or even more so if she had produced good winners in her previous litters. In the second place a breeder who is prepared to pay a stud fee of £100 is hardly likely to be so foolish as to try to economize when it comes to rearing and schooling the resultant puppies.

In short, in finally choosing the best bred dog the prospective winner selector is virtually assuring himself of the double guarantee of a good dam and more important still of sensible first-class rearing and schooling without which no greyhound is likely ever to develop the inherent potential that was bred into it.

To sum up, the time may yet come when the breeding in greyhound racing will be as significant a factor in the exercise of winner spotting as it is on the Turf. That time will only come when the same degree of thought and research has been devoted to the selective breeding of dogs as it has to horses.

But that time is not yet to hand. Even then it may still be an overstatement to say that breeding can be relied upon to the *same* extent as the assessment of a dog's performance, i.e. its form, or even to the same extent as its conformation and physical fitness. But breeding does at least provide the perceptive student of greyhound racing with another filter through which to test the mass of information presented by the race card in his search for those nuggets of valuable information.

To recapitulate, most greyhound racing fans would be giving evidence of their practical sense of proportion by regarding breeding as yet merely a background to backing in greyhound racing. It is not at present an influential factor in itself.

10

How to pick Winners: on Class

It will not have escaped the notice of the perceptive reader that in addition to the column reserved for a dog's Current Grading Figure in the form charts (page 74) there is also a column reserved for its Class or Grade. He will also have noticed that the Current Grading Figure, unlike class, may change from time to time. Clearly as a young dog gains racing experience, as it becomes more accustomed to the contours of the track, as it develops in strength or recovers from injury, so too is it logical that its times and performances consistently improve. The alert racegoer would ensure that his Current Grading Figure for the dog reflected the improvement inherent in, say, its last four outings.

To quote a practical example, it would not be unusual for an up and coming puppy which, after its first three trials and a few races, had been allotted a Current Grading Figure of say 30·70, suddenly to get the racing idea and improve quite dramatically in its next four outings to record a sequence of times 30·50, 30·40, 30·27, 30·15. In such circumstances, within a month the student, if he wanted his readings to be up to date and realistic, would be obliged to amend that dog's C.G.F. in his charts to something in the neighbourhood of 30·30. Moreover he might well feel obliged, if the dog was really up and coming, to amend it again within an equally short period.

As I stressed in an earlier chapter a dog's C.G.F. should reflect not its best ever time, not its time in a trouble-fraught race, nor when the going was either flying fast or deadly slow, but rather the time that it could be expected to record in normal conditions. Although its C.G.F. is not even its average time in a mathematical sense, it would be misleading to deny that a certan amount of averaging and levelling out is involved in any rational determination of a C.G.F.

So much then for the C.G.F. column, but what of the class column? At the outset it is important to stress that there is a greater element of permanence in the conception of class. Certainly it is more long-lived and less susceptible to change than the C.G.F. In fact a dog's class remains with it over a period of time – maybe as long as a year. A winner of the Greyhound Derby, or the St Leger, for instance, a winner of the Hollywood or the St Petersburg or Taunton Derby, does not drop from top Class A A to Class B or C just because it has not recovered quickly from some injury. It is still a top class dog unable to reproduce top class form. Its C.G.F., more sensitive to and reflecting current performances, might well be changed three or four times in that period.

An Open race dog, a classic winner, is clearly a top class dog, Class A, even when it is registering consistently slower times because for instance it is recovering from injury. It is still a Class A dog even though its current grading figure may have been written down from 29·20 to 30·10. It is only when it becomes apparent that it is never again going to recover its old standard form that its class calls for amendment.

One has but to consider the methods by which a dog's class is determined to see that this is unavoidable. One of the simplest methods of classifying a racing greyhound is by reference to the times that it records, by reference to its own C.G.F. In Chapter 6 dealing with the Racing Manager's compilation of a race card I suggested that initially at any rate he proceeded on the basis of compiling Race 1 for dogs whose C.G.F.s were within a time band of say 30·30 to 30·60, Race 2 from dogs whose C.G.F.s were within the time band of 30·00 to 30·30 and so on.

It soon became apparent to the critical racegoer that his task was not just as simple as that. In addition to the sheer mathematical assessment the Racing Manager had to have regard to many other factors – the dog's style of running, whether it was a railer or a wide runner, a fast trapper or slow starter, a fader or strong finisher, to say nothing of such material factors as the effect of the trap draw and the effect of the going on its likely performances.

There can be no denying that the class like the grade to which any racing greyhound is assigned in the intital resort is largely influenced by the times it has recorded. But just as clearly there are other factors which have a bearing on its appropriate class, not the least of which are the results of its racing performances. Certainly any entry in the class column of form charts must reflect the merit and significance of its recent performances and particularly its winning runs.

At this stage the aspirant to greyhound racing expertise may well ask the purpose of classifying a dog as Class A, Class B or Class C. What purpose does a class figure serve that is not already covered by its current grading figure? The answer broadly is that a process of classification is largely a matter of convenience. It is a systematic and orderly method of grouping and facilitates specific reference. It is easier to run down a list of dogs picking out those marked B than it is to pick out and group dogs whose times are within a certain time band.

As for the practical significance of class, one need refer no further than to the oldest of all racing sayings, 'Class will tell'. That there is a wealth of wisdom in the phrase is beyond dispute. But like so many other truisms its truth is all too often obscured by doubts as to just what it means.

Basically the adage 'Class will tell' means not that an animal capable of 30·10 will always beat one capable of 30·25, but rather that an animal that has attained a very high racing capability will in the long run show up best in lower competition even though its own record of performances have resulted in its being down-graded. Or, to put it more concisely, a dog that was once in the highest A Class even when it has come down in the world, when it is but a shadow of its former self, is still more likely to win a race against Class C rivals even if their current form seems superior.

Class in short reflects a dog's capability even though it may only give fleeting and inconsistent evidence of it. Its C.G.F. denotes the performance that it can reasonably be expected currently to give. Being longer lasting and less susceptible to frequent change the determination of a dog's class as distinct from its C.G.F. has some attraction for those who are not as diligent as the dedicated student in his search for winners.

Anyone who has followed his exercises to date will appreciate that there is no limit to the time and trouble that a dedicated professional is prepared to devote to the solution of the puzzle posed by the Racing Manager on a race card. He knows that the time devoted to the regular upkeep of form, the weekly bringing up to date of his charts, of the runners at his local track, is all well worthwhile. For him it is not merely a matter of profit but also of the pleasure he derives from solving an involved and interesting problem. For the invaluable assistance it gives him in pitting his wits against the Racing Managers and in the last resort, the bookmakers.

Some of Al Wise's friends for instance find just as much pleasure in a serious game of bridge or chess or in completing some difficult crossword puzzle. But he is at one with his friends in his admission that all such problems call for the exercise of the same intellectual faculties – patience, logic, mental honesty and above all else, objective dispassionate thought.

But he accepts that not all of his friends are as regular racegoers as he is. There are some that go but once a week, on Saturday nights maybe. For those who see only one half of the track's races, the maintenance of continuous race records is not a practical project. It is for these friends that he recommends the compilation of a Class Register on the grounds that once completed it requires less upkeep than his race records and time charts with their consequent C.G.F.s.

It is simply because the class of a greyhound is more readily determinable and, once ascertained, less mutable than a C.G.F.

that it requires infinitely less reassessment and record keeping, that it affords a reasonable alternative for those fans who prefer some more modified method, some mini course for winner finding.

If class is as influential a factor in winner finding as the pundits make out it is clearly incumbent on us to consider the various practical methods by which it can be assessed. Broadly speaking there are two methods by which class is commonly measured in greyhound racing, the Wimbledon method and the West Flagler method.

The former derives its name from the stadium where it was first applied by its Racing Manager, Con Stevens. The second derives its name from the West Flagler track where it was first applied by its Racing Manager, Tom Benner.

At Wimbledon the practice is to give the class letter A to 500 yard races, the class letter S to 700 yard races and the Class letter H to hurdles races. In each of these classes there is a further numeric classification of 1 for top class, 2 for second class, 3 for third class and so on. The bottom grade for A and S races being A10 and S10 respectively with hurdle class declining to H6. Although these classifications are basically determined on a time basis, (that is, by C.G.F.), they are then modified and kept up to date by other than purely time factors, i.e. by an assessment of the value of competitive performances.

For instance, at Wimbledon in conjunction with this class figure Con Stevens used a points system which allots to each greyhound points for every race depending upon the class of the race and the dog's position at the finish. For instance, in a Class A(1) race the winner may be allotted 15 points, the second 14, the third 13, and so on. The winner of a Class A(2) race may be awarded 14 points, the second 13 and so on. The practical advantage of such a system is that by averaging the points scored by a greyhound in, say, their last four races, the Racing Manager can get a very good idea of the general class of the greyhounds involved.

Under such a system it would clearly be illogical to put a winner of its last three Class A8 races (points 24) in the same race as a dog that has been third in his last three races in a Class

A4 race (points 30). Or to put it another way a dog with the highest points total for its last four runs would generally speaking represent a better winning chance than a dog with a low points total for the same outings.

The practical significance of such a system is that a dog's performance is evaluated but only *in relation to the calibre of the dogs against which it was competing*. A win may be a win but some wins are more significant than others! A most important factor if one takes into account just how dangerous and misleading a fast time recorded in a poor class can be.

As for the Benner system of classification which takes its name from Tom Benner, who incidentally was the originator of the format and layout of the comprehensive form guides that appear in all our race cards today, it is only fair to stress that this is indeed an *official* system. Unlike the United Kingdom where the classification outlined above – the Wimbledon system – is only adopted by some of the more progressive Racing Managers as a personal and private aid for their duties, the Benner system of classification is official and universally adopted in the States. So much so that grading and race compilation there is done to a set of Rules and Regulations that are known to and available to every racegoer. There is no room in the States for the inspired guesswork or hunch that so-and-so has been dropped in class. It is apparent from the official race card.

In short, American race cards as a matter of routine incorporate the class symbol for each runner in the same way as they do its recent times, weight and position. The practical significance of this for the winner spotter is that it highlights those dogs that have been raised or dropped in class.

To the extent that a dog's classification strictly depends upon its efforts – its successes and failures – in racing competition, the method has not inaptly been termed a 'self grading system' which incorporates a six-grade tier of capability ranging from the top Class A to B, C, D, E and M (maiden). All tracks there are required to print the following Grading Regulations on their Track Programmes:

Rule 1.13

1 The racing secretary shall be responsible for proper grading of greyhounds under provision of this section. Before the opening of a racing meet, the racing secretary, after sufficiently schooling all greyhounds, and considering their past performances, shall classify and assign them to their proper grades.

2 There will be six grades of greyhounds indicated by A, B, C, D, E and M (Maiden).

3 Any greyhound, racing in Grade E, for four (4) consecutive starts that fails to finish 1st 2nd, 3rd, or 4th in those four starts, shall be dropped from further racing at that meeting.

4 The winner of a maiden race shall be advanced no higher than Grade D.

5 The racing secretary may re-classify a greyhound at any time within its first three starts, but not more than one grade higher or lower.

6 Greyhounds falling in a race shall be considered starters in that race.

7 Greyhounds not racing on account of illness or injury for thirty (30) or more days may be reclassified.

8 Greyhounds transferring from one track to another during the racing season, shall remain in the same grade unless schooled and reclassified in accordance with the provisions of this section.

9 The winner of any race is advanced one grade until reaching Grade A.

10 If a greyhound fails to finish 1st, 2nd or 3rd in three consecutive starts (except in Grade D) or fails to earn more than one 3rd in four consecutive starts in the same grade that greyhound may fail to finish 1st, 2nd, 3rd or 4th in four consecutive starts before being lowered.

The working of this American grading system can be best illustrated by Figure 11: It will repay careful study.

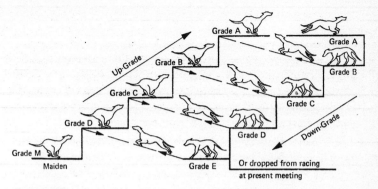

Figure 11

It will be noted that a greyhound climbs the ladder when he is on the up grade and comes down the ladder when he is on the down grade. But at any time in his racing career whether on the up or down grade he can still cross over from one grade to another depending upon his performances. Clearly not every dog has the inherent talent or required ability to reach the top class Grade A any more than it is the fate of all dogs to revert to the lowest grade of all, Grade E.

Every dog has a limit to its potential. When once its top speed capacity has been reached, the competitive nature of its peak inevitably brings about the sequence of defeats which start the dog on the down grade to find its true level again. It will be apparent from the illustration that when a dog reaches Grade B and then meets the defeats stipulated in Rule 10 it then moves to the down grade side of the ladder to Grade C. Should it sustain three losses in Grade C it would be further down graded to Grade D. If at this point conditions change and in the following race it finishes first then this result will move it back to the up grade side of the ladder to Grade C and so on.

The attraction of this system is that it is self grading. Each greyhound by virtue of its own performances determines its appropriate grade by its wins and losses in racing competition.

Broadly the Rules are applied in this way. When a dog begins its racing career it is in the Maiden Grade. After winning a race in competition it is elevated to Grade D and it never returns to Grade M again. Henceforth as the dog improves it is up graded from D to C to B into A and then into the top grade of all, AA. As a dog fails and is on the down grade it passes from AA to A and B to C with E as the bottom grade. If a dog fails in Grade E competitions it is barred from further racing at that particular track for the duration of the season.

There can be no doubt that the Benner system has comprehensively simplified what was previously a most complex subject. Moreover, it has removed the wraps of mystery and secrecy from grading and made it intelligible to the rank and file of greyhound racing.

In this connection it is noteworthy that the Benner system is universally applied throughout the States and is operated with all the force of official regulations. The principles governing the rise and decline in the grade of any dog is set out in the rules of the supervising governmental agency, which moreover are published and periodically reviewed.

It is to these systems that Al Wise draws the attention of those less dedicated than himself to a study of form and C.G.F.s. By adopting either the Wimbledon or American system – or some variation or modification thereof – it is possible to compute a class or grade figure for every dog at one's local track. Forearmed with this invaluable information the punter is distinctly better equipped than the whimsical fanciful fans to solve the problem the Racing Manager has set when he compiled his race programme.

We have seen how he has used his study and records of form and fitness to help him crack the Racing Manager's puzzle, to try to identify the dogs in a race with the best winning chance. We have seen too how as a subsidiary test he enlists a study of breeding to enable him to decide between two otherwise equal dogs, and now by a study and record of comparative class he has yet another key to the problem.

If Al Wise subscribes fully to the old saying, 'Class will tell', it is only because he knows full well that it pays to follow a dog that has been dropped in class. It is for this reason that he recommends as a mini course for the less dedicated but aspiring winner spotters the compilation and maintenance of a Class Record.

By intelligent application of this class record he can easily identify the three or four dogs on the night's card that are running out of their customary class. It may be a dog with disappointing current Grade A form racing in Grade B for the first time, or a Grade C dog racing in a Grade D race. In both cases the only evidence may be that they ran a disappointing race last time out. Coupled possibly with the fact that the Racing Manager has had an extra Grade A dog or two recently drafted into his kennels which he must initially include in his top Grade A race.

Those readers who have assimilated this exposition of the attributes of class will appreciate that one, or even two, disappointing performances is no valid reason for an alteration of a dog's *class*. In this connection it is noteworthy that in the Benner system a dog has to run disappointingly in *three* or even *four* races (Rules 4 to 10) before it is lowered one grade let alone in class.

Conceivably too, in the same race the student who has kept his class record up to date will recognize that in a particular Class B race there may be a dog or even two that have been raised in class. Dogs that are Class C but which on the strength of a winning run last time out have been up graded.

The application of a logical class test to this race will, in addition to highlighting the one dropped in class as having a better than normal chance of winning, also suggest for elimination the one or even two raised in class which have less than a normal chance of winning.

Any test, be it Form, Fitness, Family or Class, which assists the racegoer to reduce the number of *possible* winners, while raising some to the category of *probables* (the ones that he rates with a better than normal chance of winning), is the real key to profitable greyhound racing.

11

How to Bet

So far, the astute racegoer's efforts have been largely directed to identifying those dogs with the best winning chances. In addition to a study of their form, fitness, family and class, this has involved a consideration of the track characteristics, the trap draw, and even the thought processes of the Racing Manager who compiled the race.

But there is another factor to be taken into account if our friend is to capitalize to the fullest extent on his considered selections. He has already given a clue to this factor in his insistence on obtaining 'value for money' before he puts his money at hazard. One of the first lessons he learned once he had become well-versed in analysing a race and making a considered selection, was that a dog with an outstanding chance of success is not necessarily an attractive betting proposition.

A betting proposition! This conception goes to the heart of all punting, be it on the Turf or on the greyhound track. To appreciate it one must understand the workings and indeed the complexities of the betting market for it is here that the punter must necessarily buy the odds which he considers are commensurate with the degree of risk of his selection.

As for those who consider a study of the betting market an unnecessary chore, I would but add that if any game commands one's interest it is but common sense to try to learn as much as possible about the game before one plays it. One does not have to be a card sharp to play a good game of bridge, any more than one need be a race track tout to understand the mechanics of the betting market.

To begin with first principles, it is axiomatic that there is no such thing as a certainty in racing, either on the Turf or at the Dogs. Consequently it follows that there must be an element of risk no matter how good one considers a selection may be. An odds-on favourite may well indicate the dog with the best winning chance, but it is hardly likely to appeal to punters who want value for money. An odds-on favourite simply does not represent an attractive betting proposition in any six-dog race and even less in an eight-dog race as many a penniless 'chalk-eater' in the States can vouch!

Al Wise has long since accepted the bitter truth that odds-on chances do not mean certainties. Very often they represent more of a shut out bid by the layers than an invitation to bet. Accordingly he proceeds on the basis that it is the bookmaker's job to *lay* odds and that punters who try to do so will invariably end up with burnt fingers.

But if value for money is his invariable criterion of a sound betting proposition, one can surely be forgiven for inquiring what it means. What represent value for money at greyhound racing? How does our friend in his homework arrive at his own table of value for money when he compiles his own personal forecast of the odds worth a bet? Clearly the clue is to be found in an understanding of the betting market.

In an opening chapter I stressed that the winds of change have swept away many of the hypocritical and often snobbish attitudes that for too long sought to stigmatize betting as a social evil – unless of course it was done on a credit account or in a plush Members' Casino. Today the modest punter can apply himself just as conscientiously to a study of the betting market as he did to the racing capabilities of the dogs, without any feelings of guilt or moral delinquency.

Basically, betting is nothing more than a form of buying and selling. The commodity dealt in happens to be the relevant chances of each of six dogs crossing a line ahead of the remaining five. In this market the bookmakers or the Tote do the selling, and the punters do the buying. To illustrate the meaning of value for money let us consider the following example.

In order to avoid the extremes of green inexperience and of exceptional talent – the grade of dogs usually contesting the first two and the last two races respectively – let us take the fifth race on the card. One that normally comprises some of the most genuine and consistent dogs, say of good Class B calibre. Let us further assume that the Racing Manager has graded this particular race with a view to a 'blanket finish' result. In other words a race with dogs equally graded as regards time, with wide runners allotted to traps 5 and 6 so as to ensure that each runner will have a chance to give of its unimpeded best and therefore run up to and record its own current grading time.

To highlight even further the evenness of this race the expert tipsters of the Sporting Press are equally divided in their support of each of the six runners. In such a tightly graded race what then are the mathematical odds that represent true value for money.

Mathematically, the answer is simple – each dog is opposed by five equal rivals. The odds therefore must be 5-1 against any particular dog winning. But bookmakers are not philanthropists, they are businessmen selling a commodity, providing a service, for which efforts they reasonably expect some profit. On the assumption that a 10 per cent take of turnover would represent a reasonable reward for their time and trouble, then mathematically in such a race value for money would be reflected by bookmakers' laying 9-2 the field.

In such a market if the layer takes £20 on each of the six runners his take will be $6 \times £20 = £120$. Whichever dog wins his payout will be $£20 \times 9/2 = £90$, plus £20 stake, total £110. His gross profit on the race will therefore be £10 for his trouble and expenses – a *gross* rake-off of approximately 10 per cent.

But human nature being what it is, even in such a theoretically even race the betting market seldom operates just like that. The average punter is all too prone to assess a dog's chances not from his own critical assessment of form, fitness and family as our friend Al Wise does, but from the odds that are offered! All salesmen know full well that it is a deep rooted quirk of the human character only to value something that is expensive. Betting is a luxury trade and the psychology that is applied to everyday luxury buying and selling is just as keenly exploited in betting. Layers have the psychological whip hand, they know that the best way to attract customers is to *increase* the price – which in betting parlance means cutting the odds.

Why then offer 9-2 when the customers will buy at 7-2? Laying 7-2 the field in the theoretical conditions of this particular race is tantamount to the same gross take of £120 but a pay out of £20 × 7/2 = £70 plus stake £20 = £90, which involves a gross profit of £30, approximately 25 per cent. Nice work if one can get it!

Oddly enough the profit is even larger if he also cuts the odds of two dogs, say No. 1 and No. 6 to 3-1 and 5-2. Invariably there will be a rush by those human moths unable to resist the flame to back at even less favourable odds than the totally unacceptable 7-2.

But the fault lies not with the layers but with the punters who in the first place are lazy enough to allow their selection to be influenced by the layers. In the second place they are often foolish enough to back a dog, other than their own form and fitness selection, at odds that are not commensurate with the degree of risk involved.

By keeping this 9-2 bracketing firmly in his mind as the only fair mathematical odds in a really even race, the intelligent punter will be able to spot those races where the bookmakers are virtually short changing the gullible public by such extortionate quotations as 3-1, 5-2, 7-2, 4-1, 7-2, 4-1. The profit percentage in a race of this nature is 26·6 per cent. The experienced racegoer knows full well that he must be on the lookout for just such prices as these at Bank Holiday meetings and big event meetings where there are more than the usual number of 'mugs' around.

Having made up his mind that it is an even tightly graded race and that consequently odds of nothing less than 9-2 represent value for money, the intelligent punter will simply have nothing to do with the race if the bookmakers offer nothing better than

7-2. He either sits the race out or, as we shall see later, turns to the Tote for his value for money.

But our friend has also learnt that there is another side to the coin. He has learnt that with patience the bookmaker's psychological warfare is a double-edged weapon that can be used in the punter's favour. When the layers cut the odds of, say, two of the dogs to attract the flood of mug money, not infrequently they knock out one or two of the others, say dogs No. 2 and No. 4 to 5-1 and 11-2. In a race in which he has assessed the chances of all the runners as equal, the odds now quoted on two of the field represent really good value for money.

But only a small proportion of all graded races are just as close, just as insoluble as the example quoted. Clearly in the majority of races, form, fitness, trap draw and going, all influence the likely chances of success. Consequently odds well below 9-2 will be fair and relative to the lesser risks involved.

But it cannot be overstressed that there is a world of difference between the truly close *tightly graded* race in which a case for winning can be made for every runner, and a *trouble-fraught* race in which a case cannot be made for any dog because the factors all point to bumping, baulking and fighting.

Al Wise might be prepared to bet on a runner in the former type of race as soon as he was assured of value for money at 9-2 or more. He would never be prepared to bet on the latter, no matter what the odds offered. Betting without judgement is gambling, and readers who have borne with me so far will appreciate that there is no future in that.

But there are other reasons why the layers do not go 9-2 the field even in a race of this hypothetical equality. There is hardly a race on any card, at any track, where someone does not pose as 'knowing something'. Information, or more likely misinformation, travels like wildfire on a track. Someone has heard from someone that the owner of Flaming Torch is going to 'have it off tonight'. Someone has heard from Trainer A's head lad that Rose Petal is really 'on the job tonight' – and so on.

The effect that such a whispering campaign can have on the

tip-happy punters is astonishing. A man who is prepared to bet £1 on his own selection will probably stake £2.50 if given it as a hot tip. But if he hears that a coup or a 'fiddle' may be afoot, he will stake £5! Red hot information or misinformation has *burnt more fingers than the worst runners that ever raced!*

But not Al Wise's fingers. By arranging his specific selection in odds order, by preparing his own tables of value, his own betting forecast, he can then take advantage of the emotionally inspired money that makes his own 'non-selections' shorten in price with a corresponding lengthening of the odds on his selections. Often to a point where he can happily get very good value for his money.

Knowledge of the game will determine one's own opinion of the degrees of risk. By that reasoning the sport must come first, and the sensible racegoer will accept that betting is secondary as a winner finding factor.

In those races where it is clear from the market that he cannot get his considered opinion of fair odds, he has two courses of action. He can refrain from betting on the race – which he frequently does – or he can consider betting with the Tote. For he does not subscribe to the view that the Tote has no part in the 'professional' punter's repertoire. On the grounds, no doubt, that dispassionate betting demands, as a prime essential, full knowledge of the price paid, i.e. the odds at which the punter has made his purchase. Clearly when a punter strikes a bet with a bookmaker he knows the odds and how they compare with his idea of value, and consequently how much if any he stands to win. On the Tote, some professionals claim, this vital information (how much to come) is either not available or not reliable.

Certainly when the equipment, and indicators, were more primitive, there was some validity in the argument. But on most tracks today the general information indicators of the Tote are sufficiently sophisticated and sensitive to show very accurately indeed the odds and dividends that a punter can expect to receive on a winning bet.

Our young friend therefore having rejected the prices offered by the books has only to defer his investment with the Tote until as late as possible, by which time the indicators will reflect the totals staked on each runner and the aggregate pool for the race. He can then decide whether the dividend indicated represents value for money.

Far from rejecting the Tote as a medium for profitable betting the alert punter welcomes it as an effective alternative to the Books, especially when they are playing 'hard to get'. On the other hand there are times when the Tote affords him betting facilities that the Books simply cannot match. In particular the facility to back a greyhound for a place (1 or 2) or in the States for a show (1, 2 or 3) without a consequent win commitment. To say nothing of the various combination bets that have become so popular by meeting the Pools' public's preference for long odds betting.

Having regard to all the critical thought processes involved in winner selection it is not difficult to appreciate that there are seldom more than four races in which a wise punter would select a dog with an outstanding winning chance. After inspecting the Books and considering the betting market it will be surprising if these four *selections* are not reduced to three or even two *betting propositions*.

There are of course times when his form analysis reveals two potential winners in a race and he is unable to make up his mind between the two. If the Books are laying both of them at value odds then he can overcome his dilemma by backing both. But if the Books are not laying one of the equal selections at value odds then mathematically he is in some difficulty.

It is in such circumstances that the Tote can come to the punter's assistance. The intelligent racegoer may have decided that odds of 5-2 against Blue Bird and 3-1 against Bright Lion represent fair value for money, but the odds against either of these finishing in the first two places is infinitely smaller than that. In this connection I share the views of the experts who hold that in the field of betting – horses and dogs – the odds laid to a place by the Tote in six-dog greyhound racing (and for that matter to a show 1-2-3 in US greyhound racing) represents the very best value in the whole sphere of horse and dog betting.

Faced with the problem as to which of his two selections to back when the Books are not really interested, a one half stake bet on each for a place on the Tote is invariably the shrewdest of ventures and in the long run one of the most profitable.

For those of a more venturesome speculative turn of mind the Tote has yet another inducement in the Forecast. It is true that it is difficult enough to select a winner and that therefore it must be infinitely more difficult to pick both the winner *and* the second. Nevertheless the multiplied odds are often so attractive that it can be a sensible alternative for the punter deterred by the prospect of small Tote returns for a place on one of his two selections. As a general rule it is mathematically sound to restrict one's stake in forecast betting so that it does not exceed one quarter of the total stake that one would invest on an outright winner.

If the forecast comes up – as well it might if his homework has been sound – and it has been a straight clean-run race, then the odds are usually sufficiently remunerative to evoke that loveliest of feelings, a warm inner glow of self-satisfaction. In any case win or lose, the forecast has been added fun at minimal cost, and let us not forget that that is what greyhound racing is all about.

As a person dedicated to the solution of an intriguing problem by dint of study, by application of analytical dispassionate thought, anyone who has borne with me so far would be in no doubt as to my reaction to those who fondly imagine that they have a system that not only beats the Books but also saves all the form study, all the fitness inspection, all the pedigree scrutiny and all the value for money considerations – in short all the work and study that is the only route to successful greyhound racing.

As the natural selection of a dog with an outstanding winning chance depends upon critical judgement and the ability to assess its capability and form, its ultimate selection cannot be systema-tized. No systems can select or pick out winners, all that they can do is to try mathematically to ensure that one derives the maximun mathematical advantage from any winner that may be selected

In fact it follows that all so-called systems at greyhound racing are no more than staking systems.

Although I am prepared to listen attentively to their supporters I am long enough in the tooth to know that both on the Turf and on the greyhound racing track, staking systems are only a methodical way of losing money! Inevitably all staking systems which involve an increase in outlay with successive bets – no matter how modest – all break down on one common snag, the difficulty, amounting to the impossibility, of beating the long losing run.

One has but to consider one of the most common betting systems, that of backing the favourite to win a definite sum plus previous losses. This seems rational enough if one is prepared to put money at hazard on the probability of at least one favourite winning each night. But what of the night when only one favourite wins and that a joint favourite? Even more so, what of the night when all eight are beaten? The losses incurred will probably wipe out all the profits made over the course of several weeks.

The fallacy of staking systems can be most neatly exploded by taking as a practical example a staking system which has proved profitable over a period of, say, thirty bets. With the identical number of bets and winners, a nice profit can be turned into a heavy loss if the winners had merely turned up in a different order. Nothing demonstrates so effectively how disastrous any staking system can be when a real losing sequence comes along.

As far as I am concerned, systems are for the needy and the greedy, which is probably why they are still needy and greedy! Far too many racegoers lose the real enjoyment of greyhound racing by being too anxious to win – and that goes for all system followers.

12

The Hall of Fame

In this, the final chapter, it may be fitting to cast back and take stock of those factors that the student aspiring to make his interest in greyhound racing both pleasurable and profitable, has been encouraged to consider.

First and foremost there was the question of understanding the manifold capabilities and characteristics, traits and talents of the principal actor of the scene, the racing greyhound itself. Learning to recognize and assess the significance of fast trapping, railing, chasing and fading, and their effect upon a dog's chances of giving of its best or even of winning a particular race.

Then there was the matter of the contour and condition of the track itself. Whether it was sharp and tight or broad and galloping, whether the surface was turf, sand/loam, etc. Again with special reference to the aptitude or inaptitude of certain runners to give of their best in such conditions.

Then there was the matter of learning to read a race – to note the salient and significant happenings at the various focal points in the race. Again with special reference to the extent that those happenings may prevent some of the runners from giving of their best and indeed may possibly affect the result of the race.

Only when the student had acquired a sound understanding of the background of greyhound racing was he initiated into the art of selecting those dogs with the best winning chances by reference to the two most influential factors – form and fitness.

In this connection readers will recall the instruction and advice on how to compile and regularly maintain those records of dogs' performances which constitute their Form. More important still he will bear in mind the necessity of dispassionate and objective analysis if worthwhile and indeed profitable conclusions are to be drawn from that form. If he has an 'eye for an animal' he will find it easy to spot those many signs of physical well-being and the countless manifestations of a racing animal when it feels really good and rarin' to race for sheer *joie de vivre*.

Finally there was the question of acquiring a working knowledge of the market in which he was going to pit his judgement of a dog's chances against the professionals, the betting market. For it is here that the profit or loss on his interesting pastime will ultimately depend. It is with the Books or the Tote that he will put his judgement to the test 'to win or lose it all'. It is here in this final resort if he is to enjoy the sport as a pastime and to pursue it as a profitable medium, where he must be governed by the two cardinal principles.

The first is not to stake more than he can cheerfully afford to lose. The second is not to bet unless the odds represent value for money.

I have not the slightest doubt that the inclusion at this final stage in a work dedicated to the practical pursuits of winner finding, of the records of long dead greyhounds – no matter how famous – may cause the faithful student to look askance. I can only hope that if he bears with me a little longer he may come to realize its practical and even profitable significance.

In any of the walks of life that call for the exercise of human judgement, the formulation of standards by which to measure relative degrees of ability is surely inevitable. It takes little intellectual effort to appreciate that in greyhound racing everything is relative to the background against which it is staged.

One cannot attend any greyhound racing meeting without overhearing fans discussing the prospects of the dogs in, say, the first race, describing No. 1 as a fast trapper, No. 3 as having early pace, No. 6 as a strong finisher, and no doubt the description is apt in that class of race. But the practical issue for future reference on the Form Chart notes is surely just *how* fast a trapper, what *degree* of early pace, *how* strong a finisher?

To illustrate the relativity angle one has but to choose a night when there is a good class prestige Open at one's local track and compare the times to the first bend in that race with the times clocked in, say, the first and last graded races on the card. The result will more than confirm the salient truth that fast trapping and early pace, like so many other racing capabilities, are relative to the class of dog involved. The so-called fast trapping dog with early pace in Race 1 would have been last by some three or four lengths to the bend in Race 8. The fast early pace trapper in Race 8 would have brought up the rear some lengths adrift if contesting the Open race.

It is all so patently a question of class, and the best understanding of class is through a mental library of well chosen standards. Which leads to the inevitable question as to where one starts in forming greyhound racing standards. The answer is as pertinent as it is brief. At the top. The only reliable test is the degree of ability and the quality of the very best, of the really great performers of the sport. With their standards firmly engraved in one's mind one can then use them as a yardstick against which to measure and assess the calibre and characteristics of their less talented kin.

Only by casting one's mind back to some of the great trackers of yesteryear, only by watching and noting the brilliant efforts of the current stars of today's racing firmament, can one appreciate just how fast some dogs can hit the box, just how quickly they can accelerate, just how balanced they can run the bends, just how cleverly they can avoid and indeed escape trouble, and just how strongly they can sustain their racing effort.

But, above all, this study of the sport's finest and greatest performers, far from being a theoretical, historical or even nostalgic exercise, will afford racegoers perhaps the greatest and most important clue to the one quality that urges some competitors to drive themselves through all the throes of physical exhaustion, not merely in greyhound racing but in all forms of competitive racing.

I am not being cynical but merely realistic when I say that it is only a very small proportion of humans, horses or hounds, who are really prepared to crucify their bodies in racing competition. What is it for instance that will drive some amateur athlete to undergo a training process of galloping for miles over sticky plough and wearing heavy boots, while his fellow is prepared to jog around a few simple laps of a cinder track?

The longer one frequents the racing scene, the more deeply one becomes involved in it, the more closely one associates with such experienced officials as Racing Managers, trainers and breeders of racing livestock the more difficult it becomes to escape the conclusion that the physical variations of racing greyhounds (and probably humans and horses too) are not of themselves the answer to the disparity in their racing ability.

The physical equipment of two greyhounds can be absolutely identical, with the same weight, height, conformation, pulse rate, and so on. They may even be litter brothers reared together, prepared by the same trainer, and yet one may well be a dog of national repute while the other can hardly run fast enough to keep itself warm, hard put in fact to make the grade in the first race on the same track on which his brother is the record holder.

As the answer to this discrepancy, this gulf between two identical dogs, can hardly be physical, then by inference it must be either nervous or mental. In free company with others, some dogs are irresistibly activated by a driving urge to outstrip them, to reach the quarry first in gallop – whether it be a scrap of windborne paper, a lark slowly spiralling up from the meadow or a hare loping over the stubble. But others are just as happy to lollop in company with their fellows – almost loth to leave them behind.

Throughout the age-old history of coursing there have been many attempts to define this quality to strive for leadership as determination, selfishness, jealousy, or even primitive destructiveness – and frankly there is a trace of all of these in the quality. In greyhound racing circles the most apt definition of the quality is probably 'the will to win'. A spirit that may well be indefinable but at least the absence of it is clearly exemplified by the 'chaser'. Certainly, without this quality no dog could possibly have attained that long consistent series of successes in the hottest of classic and prestigious competition which entitles it to be regarded as a Star in the greyhound racing firmament.

As the young student of greyhound racing graduates from his noviciate, as his horizons broaden with his knowledge of the sport, as his standards become higher and more testing, it is but natural that his increasing experience will become adorned with vivid thoughts of the great dogs whose efforts thrilled him, and probably with the happy memories of successful betting propositions.

In the course of time these current studies will become memories, but not memories to be abandoned to the realms of limbo, for the calibre of the truly great ones will remain ever green in his memory as standards against which to assess up and coming aspirants to track fame.

When he hears some promising young dog described as the fastest trapper ever, when he reads in the Press the all too frequent and all too extravagant eulogies of some up and coming puppy as the greatest sprinter ever, he will quickly be able to compare them with his own personal standard. He will be able to ask himself, 'Is it really faster out of the box than Ballynennan Moon?' and 'Is it really a greater tracker than Future Cutlet, Wild Woolley, Mile Bush Pride or Real Huntsman?' On the honest answer to these questions, his dispassionate judgement, his analytical perception will depend and, to be truthful, the profit of his betting transactions. But the more he calls upon his standards to assist him in assessing those greyhounds currently racing, the more practical it becomes that those standards be well conceived, reliable and dispassionately based.

In the States the greyhound racing fan anxious to acquire a set of standards by which to judge the dogs currently running at his local meeting, is in the fortunate position of finding that the work has already largely been done for him. In 1963 the NGA and the AGTOA established in Abilene, Kansas, a Hall of Fame dedicated to every individual – including greyhound – 'who has contributed to the advancement of the world's greatest sport'.

It is against the background of the outstanding talents of the fourteen greyhounds already elected to a place of honour in their Hall of Fame that greyhound racing men throughout the States can measure and assess the merits and talents of dogs currently aspiring to greatness in their present racing circuit.

In the United Kingdom unfortunately there has been no such official recognition of the star performers of the greyhound racing scene, no historical tribute to their exceptional talents and capabilities. Accordingly, the enthusiast seeking to add yet another tool to his equipment for cracking the puzzle the Racing Manager has set, is forced back on his own devices. It is to cater for his need, or at least to provide a basis for his own further researches, that I offer the following thumbnail sketches of dogs whose records and talents suggest that they are worthy standards of comparison.

Mick the Miller

April 1926
Brindled
Glorious Event—Na Boc Lei

Breeder: Father Brophy
Owners: Mrs A. H. Kempton, Mr A H Williams
Trainers: Mr S. J. Orton Mr P Horan
Racing Record: 61 wins in 81 starts

The first personality dog of greyhound racing. If Rural Rube put Massachusetts on the greyhound racing map in the States, then Mick the Miller put greyhound racing on the British sporting map.

The first dog to win the Greyhound Derby twice – in 1929 and 1930. He also won the Cesarewitch and the St Leger and therefore shares with Future Cutlet the record of winning four classics. He set up five track records over distances of 525, 550 and 600 yards, and still holds the British record of scoring a sequence of nineteen consecutive wins.

Not endowed with the electrifying early pace of some of his contemporaries, Mick the Miller won most of his races the hard way – coming from behind. The fact that he was in the first three in all but five of his races is proof positive of his unique ability to anticipate and therefore avoid the inevitable bumping and baulking at the bends. His ability to weave through a field was as uncanny as it was unique. Without question this was the craftiest dog ever to race in the United Kingdom.

Britain may not have a Hall of Fame, but as the dog that popularized greyhound racing in the United Kingdom it is fitting that he should now stand mounted on the first floor of the British Natural History Museum.

Future Cutlet

April 1929
Brindled
Mutton Cutlet—Wary Guide
Breeder: Mr W. Walsh
Owner: Mr W. A. Evershed
Trainer: Mr S. Probert

Like Mick the Miller Future Cutlet won four classics – the Derby 1933, the Laurels 1931 and the Cesarewitch 1931 and 1932 – and very nearly emulated Mick's double in the premier classic, for he was also runner-up to Wild Woolley in the 1932 Derby.

In appearance Future Cutlet was as handsome as Mick the Miller was plain. His silhouette has been adopted in countless racing magazines as the classic greyhound conformation. In a racing career of three seasons he won over £6000 in prize money.

A brilliantly fast trapper with electrifying acceleration. The classic 525 trip was almost certainly his ideal distance for he was inclined to fade over 600 yards. Temperamentally he was rather nervous and fretful.

Future Cutlet qualifies for the racegoer's album of standards as the perfect medium distance performer – a brilliant box hitter, with electric early pace, a neat and well balanced runner of a curve.

Wild Woolley

April 1930
Brindled
Hautby—Wild Witch
Breeder: Mr A. H. Westwood
Owner: Mr S. Johnson
Trainer: Mr J. Rimmer

Won three classics – the Derby 1932, the Laurels and Gold Collar 1933 – in addition to the Trafalgar Cup 1931 and the Northern Flat Championship 1932.

One of the greatest all-rounders of the sport – capable of winning top class sprints of up to 400 yards and also stayers' events of 700 yards – he was a natural tracker and runner of a curve. He could be taken to a strange track without a trial and not only win but even break the track record. He defeated Future Cutlet by a neck in the greatest and most exciting match ever staged.

For the book of standards Wild Woolley is a living proof of the saying that they go in all shapes and sizes, and in the sphere of racing competition it is a case of handsome is as handsome does. Certainly he did not compare with his contemporary Future Cutlet for good looks and classic conformation. An exceptionally strong and well balanced greyhound, very sure and nimble footed, Wild Woolley was never once knocked over in a long and varied racing career.

Ballynennan Moon

April 1939
Brindled
Mr Moon—Banriogan Dan
Breeder: Mr P. Britton
Owner: Mrs J. J. Cearns
Trainer: Mr S. J. Orton
Racing Record: 73 wins in 111 starts

Condemned by the accident of his birth to racing in war time,

Ballynennan Moon was denied the classic triumphs he most certainly would have gained. In normal times the Scurry Gold Cup, the Gold Collar, the Laurels and Derby would all have been well within his compass.

The measure of his toughness and versatility can be gauged by the fact that in times when transport was difficult and invariably uncomfortable, Ballynennan Moon ran and won on fourteen different tracks behind all types of hares and equipment.

He is regarded by many judges as the greatest sprinter ever. Although he won over distances up to 550 yards, his box hitting and particularly his phenomenal early pace and acceleration invariably saw him off and round the first bend – no matter from what box – well clear of his field. Virtually unbeatable over 300 to 440 yards.

For the student's record of standards, Ballynennan Moon gave the lie to the all too common and completely unjust charge that sprinters lack courage, and also the the idea that good sprinters are invariably round muscled and heavily built, for Ballynennan Moon was one of the tallest and slimmest of racing greyhounds. He was genuine to the nth degree. His consistent record bears this out. Bought in July 1941, he ran his first race in Britain on 1 August 1941 and in 79 consecutive weeks of racing competition he contested 91 events and won 65.

Mile Bush Pride

August 1956
Brindled
The Grand Champion—Witching Dancer
Breeder: Mrs M. Johnston
Owner: Mr N. W. Purvis
Trainer: Mr J. Harvey

Mile Bush Pride won the 1960 Cesarewitch, and emulated Trev's Perfection's remarkable hat-trick of winning the three national Derbies – English, Scots and Welsh – in 1959. In the course of so doing he set up a new White City record for the trip of 28·57, and also a new record for the Welsh Derby of 28·80. He scored a second classic success when he won the 1960 Cesarewitch also in track record time of 32·65. In addition he won such prestige events as the Pall Mall at Harringay, the Select Stakes and Spring Cup at Wembley, and the Ladbrooke Stakes.

Mile Bush Pride was on the racing scene at a time when ability to break the 29·00 barrier for the 525 yard trip stamped any greyhound with the classic hallmark of exceptional talent. It is true that some few managed to do so occasionally, but Mile Bush Pride, like his great contemporary Pigalle Wonder, was the only dog to reduce it to a formality. Jack Harvey's charge in fact broke 29 seconds at White City on no less than twelve occasions. When he retired from racing he held the track records at White City, Cardiff, West Ham and Harringay.

For the student's album of standards Mile Bush Pride represents the Mr Consistency of British greyhound racing – a dog of some 70 lb racing weight. For sheer beauty of conformation he was in the same class as Future Cutlet. From the point of view of temperament and constitution he was a trainer's dream for he was never sick or sorry, let alone on the injured list, for a single day in his racing life.

Pigalle Wonder

1955
Brindled
Champion Prince—Prairie Peg
Breeder: Mr T. Murphy
Owner: Mr A. L. Burnett
Trainer: Mr J. Syder

Pigalle Wonder won the Derby in 1958 in the then world record time of 28·44 seconds. He scored another classic triumph in 1958 in the Cesarewitch when he dead-heated with Rylane Pleasure. In addition he won such other prestigious events in 1958 as the Pall Mall, the London Cup, the Edinburgh Cup and the Futurist Stakes, and in 1959 the Wood Lane Stakes and Anglo Irish Cup.

Pigalle Wonder's true merit, however, cannot be gauged by the number of successes he scored but rather by the style and manner in which he secured them. At a time when most other top class trackers were striving to break the 29·00 barrier for the glory and distinction that went with it (in much the same way as athletes were trying to break the four minute mile barrier) Pigalle Wonder made it almost commonplace. At the White City he broke 29 seconds on no fewer than nineteen occasions, and what is probably more indicative of truly great ability, he broke 29·00 at the infinitely more difficult Wembley track no fewer than five times. In 1958, in fact, he held the track records at both White City and Wembley with times of 28·44 and 28·78 respectively.

When after three years of competition in the highest class he retired from the racing scene, he had no fewer than seven track records to his credit over distances ranging from 500 to 550 yards, and at tracks as distinct and different as White City, Wembley, Harringay, Carntyne and Powderhall, and had won more than £7500 in prize money.

A greyhound of truly magnificent conformation and appearance, Pigalle Wonder was that rarity, a heavyweight of some 76 lb racing weight that was so beautifully balanced and proportioned that he never *looked* big or heavy. The pundits may say in defence of the ugly ones that 'they come in all shapes and sizes' and that 'handsome is as handsome does' but Pigalle Wonder, along with Mile Bush Pride, provided living proof of the truth that the *very* fast dogs are *very* good looking.

Dolores Rocket

1968
Brindled
Newdown Heather—Comeon Dolores
Breeder/Trainer/Owner: Mr H. C. White
Racing Record: 38 wins from 64 starts

Dolores Rocket emulated the Derby triumphs of those other great bitches Greta Ranee in 1935 and Narrogar Ann in 1949 by winning the Derby in 1971. She carved a unique niche for herself in greyhound racing scrolls by adding a second classic triumph when she won the St Leger in the same year.

Her consistent racing record in 1970 and 1971 puts her on a higher plane than any of her sex, for she won among other events the Puppy Oaks in 1970 as well as the Wembley Spring Cup, the Wimbledon Spring Cup, the Essex Vase and the Kent Spring Trophy over distances ranging from 500 to 700 yards.

Dolores Rocket ranks with such famous old timers as Queen of the Suir and Quarter Day as probably the greatest bitch ever to grace the British racing scene.

For the student's album of standards, Dolores Rocket must go down as a brilliantly fast trapper with first class early pace and moreover with the ability to sustain her pace over distances up to 700 yards. The versatile genuine type of greyhound that almost certainly would have done well in the United States, she was the United Kingdom counterpart of Indy Ann and Fern Nature.

Patricia's Hope

July 1970
White and fawn

Breeder:	Mr M. Murphy
Owners:	Gordon and Basil Marks, John O'Connor and Brian Stanley
Trainers:	A. Jackson, J. O'Connor
Racing Record:	20 wins in 38 starts

By following up his victory in the 1972 Greyhound Derby with another win in 1973, Patricia's Hope emulated the 43-year-old record of Mick the Miller. Moreover, as in 1972 he had also added both the Welsh and Scots Derbies to his credit, Patricia's Hope joined Trev's Perfection and Mile Bush Pride as the only greyhounds to achieve this notable classic treble.

In the light of such a record – a classic Derby double and the supporting hat-trick – there are grounds for the view that Patricia's Hope is the most successful tracker the sport has yet produced in the United Kingdom. Certainly with a total of £27 500 stake money he is in an unassailable position as the biggest money spinner of all time. On the other hand there are those who would argue that having regard to inflation, Future Cutlet's £6000 in 1932 compares more than favourably.

Physically, Patricia's Hope was cast in the same tall, almost leggy mould of that other great tracker, Ballynennan Moon. In addition to his superb physical endowment, Patricia's Hope was blessed with a placid, almost imperturbable, disposition. An invaluable attribute when one considers the effect that travelling and strange kennels can have on a highly trained animal contesting classic and prestigious events in four countries.

A brilliantly fast trapper, especially from the outside boxes, he had a fine turn of early pace which invariably saw him clear or well placed at the first bend – a position he normally consolidated in trips up to 525 yards. His propensity for wide running and his preference for traps 5 and 6 may deny him the accolade of such complete all-round greyhounds as Future Cutlet, Pigalle Wonder and Mile Bush Pride, but his record alone establishes him as a standard by which to judge all top class 'middle distance' trackers.

Not the least notable feature of Patricia's Hope's success is the fact that he returned to win his second Derby after a year at stud during which he served 67 bitches and sired some 400 puppies. As there was a bitch Softly in the next trap to him in the Final, which moreover finished close up second to him, his performance must be regarded as a unique example of canine concentration and singleness of purpose!

So much then for the capabilities and characteristics, the traits and talents, of those great greyhounds that have graced the tracks of the United Kingdom since the inception of the sport. Dogs whose successes in the highest class of competitive racing, whose consistent record extended sometimes over a period of three years, proved beyond all doubt that in addition to physical talent and endowment they also had the most important spark of all – the will to win.

In the United States the dedicated student of greyhound racing is spared the necessity of the selection of talented trackers to serve as practical standards of tracking talent. In 1963 the greyhound racing business itself, through its National Greyhound Association and American Greyhound Track Operators Association, has elevated some fourteen greyhounds to its Hall of Fame. It is against the background of the outstanding talents of these dogs that greyhound racing men throughout the States seek to measure and assess the ability and potential of the up and coming dogs who are currently making their presence felt – be it at Wonderland, Raynham, Taunton, St Petersburg, Biscayne or Flagler.

Rural Rube

1937
Brindled
My Laddie—Lady Gangdrew

Breeder:	Mr G. Laman
Owner:	Mr R. B. Carroll
Racing Record:	51—16—10 from 81 starts, including:

The Flagler Derby	1939
The Flagler Futurity	1938
The Wonderland Inaugural	1938
The Wonderland Inaugural	1940
The Wonderland Juvenile	1938

Held two track records and one world record 5/16ths mile 31·00

In addition held the Wonderland Park record for a sequence of 19 wins in one season.

If Mick the Miller put greyhound racing on the British sporting map then Rural Rube put Massachusetts on the American greyhound racing map. One of that very rare species – a 'personality' animal.

Like Mick the Miller, Rural Rube had no set pattern or style of running. Not a brilliantly fast trapper, he usually came off the pace and would cut inside or go overland as the openings offered. His skill (like that of Mick the Miller) in picking his way through a field still remains an all-time high.

For those fans seeking to compile a library of worthwhile standards as a background to measure and compare current performers, then Rural Rube, like Mick the Miller, represents the highest possible standard for track craft and racing intelligence.

Flashy Sir

1943
Brindled
Lucky Sir—Flashy Harmony
Breeder: Hazel L. Morrison
Owner: Merrill Blair
Trainer: J. B. Hatzo
Racing Record: 60—10—4 in 80 starts, including:
                  The Biscayne Derby   1946
                  The Taunton Inaugural   1946
                  The Taunton Inaugural   1947

Probably the only greyhound in the history of the sport whose owner was paid by several tracks *not* to run him.

As befits a greyhound given the sobriquet of the Sea Biscuit of Greyhound Racing, Flashy Sir was the epitome of consistency as the following records bear out:

            11 wins out of 12 at Raynham   1945
             9 wins out of 9 at Flagler   1946
             6 wins out of 6 at Raynham   1946
            10 wins out of 12 at Raynham   1947

As the keynote of consistency is a versatile technique – an all-round racing equipment – then Merrill Blair's champion, the Mr Consistency of greyhound racing, is as fine a standard of all-round ability as the greyhound racing scene has to offer.

Real Huntsman

1948
Light brindled
Never Roll—Medora

Breeder:	Randle Brothers
Owner:	Mr Gene Randle
Racing Record:	67—9—11 in 104 starts, including:

The Flagler Futurity	1950
The American Derby, Taunton	1950
The Gold Collar, Taunton	1950
The Blue Ribbon, Taunton	1950
The American Derby, Taunton	1951
The Flagler Derby, Taunton	1951

In addition to winning some $68 000 in stake money, Real Huntsman held six separate track records and two world records over distances ranging from the Futurity's 495 to 720 yards. He is best remembered for the all-time record of 27 consecutive wins at five different tracks over every distance!

The nearest approach to an unbeatable racing machine ever to grace a greyhound racing track.

This was a dog that makes nonsense of the all too common claim of others to be the Best Greyhound Ever. For all-round perfection – fast trapping, early pace, clever running, determination and sheer machine-like consistency – Real Huntsman remains the absolute standard.

Indy Ann

1953
Brindled
Pageant—Praying Darkie

Breeder/Owner:	Mr Ed Willard
Trainer:	J. Strazicich
Racing Record:	137—37—18 from 223 starts.
	Holds the American record for the greatest

overall total of wins, 137, and also for the
most wins in any one year – 61 in 1956.
Voted by United States Sportswriters:
The Outstanding Bitch of 1955
The Outstanding Bitch of 1956
The Outstanding Greyhound of 1956

In no fewer than 149 of her 223 starts the support of her
Caliente track fans brought her odds down to less than even money.

For sheer toughness and durability the Caliente Queen must be
the perpetual standard for all breeders and racegoers. To last out
a racing career of 223 races, even in the lower, less demanding
grades, is a tribute to any dog's physical constitution, but even
more so to its mental drive and urge. To do so in the heat and fire
of Grade AA racing is almost unbelievable.

The supreme standard of toughness, durability and feminine
will to win.

Beach Comber

1945
Brindled
More Taxes—Soapy Hands
Breeder: Mr Paul Sutherland
Owner: Mr Paul Sutherland
Trainer: Sam Bush
Racing Record: 99—51—18 in 218 starts, including:
                 The Biscayne All Florida Derby   1948
                 The Biscayne All Florida Derby   1949
                 The Flagler Inaugural   1947
                 The Multnomah Au Revoir   1947
                 The Multnomah Derby   1947
                 Held the world record of 30·05 seconds for
                 Flagler's 5/16th mile course.

Dumpy in appearance, 'Shorty' was anything but a show piece,
but like Mick the Miller and Wild Woolley, Beach Comber proved
that in racing 'handsome is as handsome does'.

The type of greyhound about which one could say that he seldom if ever lost a race that he ought to have won. He certainly won scores of races where at one stage he seemed well beaten.

Beach Comber's qualities of heart and racing intelligence assures him a place in any album of standards.

Never Roll

1939
Brindled
Lucky Roll—Never Fail

Breeder:	Frank Falk	
Owner:	Mr G. A. Alderson	
Racing Record:	The Tampa Derby	1943
	The Wonderland Derby	1942
	The Wonderland Inaugural	1942
	Held four world records.	

A tight, well balanced railer, he resembled Trev's Perfection in his ability to drop on to the rail at the right moment, even from the outside trap. A fast trapper and a very fast finisher. Never Roll, like Man O' War on the Turf, gave the lie to the rule that it is impossible to make two winning runs in a race – at the start and at the finish. Apart from this unique ability he is entitled to a place in any album of standards as proof positive that breeding does count, that blood and class will out, for Never Roll was bred in the purple, by the Hall of Fame sire Lucky Roll, and he was himself the sire of two other Hall of Fame sons, Lucky Pilot and Real Huntsman.

Fern Nature

1939
Brindled
My Laddie—Lady Gangdrew

Breeder:	Glenn Laman	
Owner:	Mr R. B. Carroll	
Racing Record:	The Flagler Derby	1941
	The Flagler Derby	1942

The Flagler Derby   1943
The Flagler Futurity   1942
The Biscayne Derby   1943
The Miami Inaugural   1941
The Miami Inaugural   1942

As the only greyhound ever to win three consecutive Derbies, Fern Nature's place in the scrolls of greyhound racing fame is assured. For a dog to retain his racing prowess for three whole seasons and be able to concede age first to his elders and finally to his juniors and defeat them in classic competition is remarkable enough (compare Spanish Battleship's famous hat-trick in the Irish Derbies of 1953, 1954 and 1955), but for a bitch with all the imponderable effects of seasonal variations, then such an accomplishment is almost beyond belief. On this score alone, Fern Nature probably serves in the book of standards as the greatest bitch of all time. Certainly in conjunction with Indy Ann, Fern Nature represents the standard by which all bitches must be judged before they can claim to be 'great'.

As a younger sister of the legendary Rural Rube, breeders will be entitled to add by way of explanation, 'The right blood was there'.

Lucky Pilot

1944
Brindled
Never Roll—Dixie By
Owner: Mr Ray Holmes
Trainer: Mr Ray Holmes
Racing Record: 61—13—7 in 92 starts, including:
                 The St Petersburg Inaugural   1947
                 The Wonderland Inaugural   1946
                 The Wonderland Inaugural   1948

The holder at one time of no fewer than four track and world records at Wonderland. Like his counterpart in Britain, Wild

Woolley, Lucky Pilot could adapt himself with brilliance to sprint middle or long distances. Examine his times:

18·10 seconds for the 3/16ths trip   330 yards
27·40 seconds for the Futurity trip   495 yards
30·40 seconds for the 5/16ths trip   550 yards

Like Wild Woolley's matches with Future Cutlet which thrilled racegoers in the United Kingdom, Lucky Pilot's five match races with Flashy Sir thrilled the fans at Flagler and St Petersburg in 1947. The fact that in four of these five matches the track record was broken, supports the view that from the point of view of sheer quality and class such a series has never been equalled either before or since.

So much then for the great stars whose thrilling efforts so brilliantly illuminated the greyhound racing firmaments in the United Kingdom and the United States of America. The sporting world has good cause to be indebted to them. Not only for setting the standards by which to judge and assess up and coming current dogs, but also for the contribution they made – albeit unwittingly – towards the popularity of greyhound racing.

There are scores of examples throughout the wide spectrum of the entertainment industry of the promotion of interesting and even exciting spectacles which never quite achieve popular appeal. So much so that now it is commonly accepted that there must be some ingredient other than technical interest and excitement if the project is to appeal to the popular sporting imagination.

The key to the secret of popularity in the world of sporting entertainment seems to lie in the extent to which the public begin to feel some personal association, almost affection, for the performers themselves. There are those, and I am one of them, who hold that it is this feeling that goes to the very heart of real 'popularity'.

The examples are legion. Jack Hobbs and Loll Larwood in cricket; Babe Ruth and Joe di Maggio in baseball; Bobby Jones and Jack Nicklaus in golf; Gordon Richards and Johnny Longden in racing; Jack Dempsey and Jimmy Wilde in boxing; Bobby Moore and Bobby Charlton in football. But the cult of personality as a potent factor in popularity does not end there. The mere mention of such names as Brown Jack, Mill Reef and Brigadier Gerard, of Golden Miller and Arkle, of Man o' War, Sea Biscuit, Citation, Kelso and Secretariat, conjures up memories, and affection too, that assure their place as characters in the hearts of sporting thousands. Moreover, by so doing, they made a substantial contribution to the popularity of both the British and the American racing scenes.

So too in greyhound racing, the character and personality of such stars as Mick the Miller, Future Cutlet, Ballynennan Moon and Pigalle Wonder in Britain, and Mission Boy, Snappy Joe, Rural Rube, Beach Comber and Real Huntsman in America, assured not only lasting affection and popularity for themselves but also for the sport of greyhound racing which they so richly adorned.

Glossary A:

Race Card Abbreviations (*UK and USA*)

A or AA	Highest grade of race	F.A.	Fast away
A.R.T.	Actual Running Time	Fl.	Fell
B.	Bitch	F & W.	Fawn and white
B	Grade of race – second highest	H.	Hurdle race
Bd.	Brindled	Hd.	Head
Bd & W.	Brindled and white	I.	Impeded
Bk.	Black	M	Grade – Maiden
Bk & W.	Black and white	Ns.	Nose
Blkd.	Blocked or Baulked	Nk.	Neck
Bmpd.	Bumped	Pchd.	Pinched
C	Grade of race – middle	Prom.	Prominent
Clsng.	Closing	S.A.	Slowly away
Crwd.	Crowded	Shufld.	Shuffled
D	Grade of race – second lowest	Stpd.	Stopped
D.	Dog	T.	Trial race
D.H.	Dead Heat	W.	Wide
Dist.	Distance	Wt.	Weight
D.N.F.	Did not finish	Wkned.	Weakened
E	Grade of race – lowest	W & Bk.	White and black
F.	Fawn	W & Bd.	White and brindled

Glossary B:

Racing Terms (UK and USA)

Alert	Fast tracker from starting box
All the Way	Never headed – always in front – see Box to Wire
Almost Up	Just fails to win in last stride
Baulked	To be impeded by another dog – see Blocked
Beat Box	Takes big lead by breaking fast
Bear Out	To carry another greyhound wide during race
Bertillon	Established system of identification
Blanket	Dog's covering bearing number, colour and position in race – see Jacket
Blocked	Shut off when trying to move up
Box to wire	To lead throughout the race – see All the Way
Broke stride	To shorten stride and lose ground – see Off-strided
Bumped	To be hit by another dog
Break	Start of a race
Come Again	Moved up after dropping back
Checked	To hesitate or prop – shorten stride during race
Closed fast	To finish with a rush
Close Quarters	Racing close together – lacking racing room
Drawing Away	Increased lead in home stretch
Early foot	High speed of a greyhound in first stages of a race
Faded	Dropping back
Falter	To run uncertainly – to hesitate or waver
Flash	Brief moment of good speed
Fly the Turn	To veer out sharply on a turn – losing ground to other greyhounds on inside
Form	Record of past performances
Going Away	Steadily drawing away from field – see Drawing Away

Good Effort	Tried hard, game attempt, not good enough
Green	Inexperienced
Handily	To win without being pressed – without apparent effort
Hug Rail	To take shortest route, close to rail – see Rail Runner
Impeded	To be hindered from giving best effort by crowding, interference, bumping, etc.
Jacket	Dog's covering bearing number, colour and position in race – see Blanket
Just Up	Gets up in last stride to win
Knocked Back	Forced back after collision with another runner
Left	Leaves box very slowly
Lumber	Too much flesh
Maiden	Greyhound that has never won a race
No factor	Trailing – never in real contention
Off-strided	Momentarily loses reduced stride and balance
Outrun	Good effort but unable to keep pace with others
Place	Finish 2nd in a race
Pinched Back	Crowded and forced to drop back
Prop	To hesitate or slow down during race – see Checked
Rough Trip	Crowded or blocked several times in race
Rail Runner	Dog that runs close and tight to rail – see Hug Rail
Router	Greyhound with ability to run distances in excess of Futurity – see Stayer
Saved Ground	Raced on inside, near rail
Show	Finish 3rd in a race
Shut Off	Blocked when trying to move up
Shuffled Back	To be so crowded and impeded as to lose considerable ground
Stayer	A greyhound able to sustain racing speed over distances in excess of 3/8 mile (650 yards) – see Router
Stretch Drive	Extra effort in final home straight
Strip	Actual racing track surface .
Trailed	To run well in the rear of the field
Weakened	To be unable to sustain effort after showing good speed
Wire	The finishing line of a race

Appendix 1:

Do's and Don'ts of Successful Betting

1   **Do not bet more than you can cheerfully afford to lose.**

2   Do not exceed the amount you have set aside for your night's entertainment.

3   Do not lose the enjoyment of the sport by being too anxious to win.

4   Do be as afraid of backing losers as you are of missing winners.

    Do not bet more than you can cheerfully afford to lose.

5   Do not bet on a race unless you can obtain value for money.

6   Do not forget that gambling only starts where thinking stops.

7   Do not let long odds put you off your considered selection. If you feel confident, bet confident. If you feel tepid, bet timid.

8   Do not overplay your stake on short priced favourites.

    Do not bet more than you can cheerfully afford to lose.

9   Do not forget that odds on chances do not represent certainties or even good things.

10 Do not mix up your bets – wins, places, shows, forecasts, etc. Mixing the hopeful and fanciful with considered selections dilutes the reward of study.

11 Do keep in mind that when it comes to betting, a pound of performance is worth a stone of information.

12 Do not forget that information – misinformation – has burnt more fingers than all the worst runners that ever raced.

    Do not bet more than you can cheerfully afford to lose.

13 Do remember that study and judgement always overtake luck in the long run.

Appendix 2:

Hints for Winner Spotters

1 **Have you done your homework thoroughly – studied your Form Charts, etc.?**

2 Have you refined your Form selections to a hard-core residue of, say, four for the meeting?

3 Have you noted for special consideration those bitches approaching their 17th/18th week out of season but who have not yet 'sprung'?

4 Have you considered the state of the track, e.g. the effect of the heavier going on the rails and the better going on the outside?

5 Have you further reviewed your Form selections in the light of their appearance on parade, i.e. their Fitness?

Have you done your homework thoroughly – studied your Form Charts, etc.?

6 Have you given the benefit of the doubt to the fast trapper and railer, rather than the slow starter and strong finisher?

7 Have you given sufficient credit to the improvement potential in an up and coming puppy who won last time out?

8 Have you taken into account that in winter racing on peat nine out of ten winners are in the lead at the first bend?

9 Have you considered the effect on your Form selections if they are racing under lights for the first time?

10 Have you kept in mind that a dog can usually be relied upon to find about 0·30 seconds after a trial on a strange track?

Have you done your homework thoroughly – studied your Form Charts, etc.?

Listed below are a selection of titles available from Gamblers Book Services on Greyhound Racing. We have over 300 more titles available on other aspects of Gambling including Poker, Blackjack, Roulette, Horse Racing, Sports Betting, Football. If you would like a complete catalogue please send your details to G.B.S. (Dept WAGR), 18 Coleswood Rd, Harpenden, Herts, AL5 1EQ, England.

In addition we run the OLDCASTLE GREYHOUND CLUB, which gives its members an opportunity to own a share in a string of greyhounds at a minimal once off cost of ONLY £100. At present the club owns dogs racing at Wembley (26% win rate — including 3 opens), Hackney (46% win rate) and Wimbledon (33% win rate). If you would like further information write to Dept OGC at the above address.

Number e.g. 56 = page extent; letters, e.g. st = type of binding; st = stapled, wi = wiro, pb = paperback, hb = hardback.

RACING GREYHOUNDS
52994 75577 £7 56 st Pico Publishing
Monthly U.S. magazine for greyhound handicapping. Many articles on various different handicapping methods, some with U.S. bias but often very relevent for U.K. and Ireland. 12 Issues yearly. £65 for 12 or £35 for 6 inc. P & P.

THE GREYHOUND HANDICAPPER Adams, Earl
0961274824 £9.95 72 wi Earl Adams
Read and correctly interpret key data from past races, identify winning signals, "smart money", time handicapping exotic bets. U.S. bias but still useful.
INTERMEDIATE/ADVANCED

LET'S GO TO THE GREYHOUND RACES
Anderson, Jerry
£8.95 80 pb Gold
Shows basics of reading racecard, handicapping advice,
how to analyse a race, betting procedures and money
management. Includes test races. U.S. bias and a little
amateurish but still useful.
ALL LEVELS

GEORGE CURTIS: TRAINING GREYHOUNDS
Barnes, Julia
0948955104 £14.95 220 hb Ringpress
Fascinating insight into the man that rose from the
slums of pre-war Portsmouth to become one of the
leading greyhound trainers. Invaluable for all owners,
breeders, trainers and fans.
ALL LEVELS

GREYHOUND FACT FILE (1991 EDITION)
Barnes, Julia
0948955619 £7.99 432 pb Ringpress
Useful guide to a variety of information covering all
aspects of greyhound racing, throughout the world, track
and coursing, NGRC and Independent. Revised and
updated with many new pictures. Very useful and good
value.
ALL LEVELS.

GUIDE TO GREYHOUND RACING & BETTING
Bennett, David
0901091081 £4.95 128 pb Sporting Life
How to bet, who to bet with, how to understand form
and estimate winning chances. Facts about times, odds
and betting systems. Good basic introduction.
BASIC

SPORTING LIFE GREYHOUND ANNUAL 1990-91
Betts, Bob
0901091332 £4.95 144 pb Sporting Life
Useful guide covering British and Irish track facts, track
records, big race winners, breeding, training and betting
features, racing fixtures.
ALL LEVELS

OWNING A RACING GREYHOUND Beumer, Johanna
090109126X £4.95 96 pb Sporting Life
Covers the forms of racing, development of a greyhound,
becoming an owner, the racing years, retirement of dog,
"a day in the life of a greyhound". Useful background
reading.
ALL LEVELS

SYSTEMS DON'T WORK AT GREYHOUND TRACKS
Black, C. Linzey
£8.95 40 pb Black
Aimed at slightly more advanced punters with emphasis
on strictly applying speed factors. A dozen outside
systems are analysed and are shown why they failed.
U.S. bias.
INTERMEDIATE

PHYSIOTHERAPY IN VETERINARY MEDICINE
Bromiley, Mary
0632028335 £13.95 136 pb Blackwell
Of use to Greyhound (and Horse) racing trainers,
covering massage, magnetic field therapy, ultrasound,
laser therapy, etc. with substantial section by Paddy
Sweeney. Use only under vet's guidance.
ADVANCED

THE WINNING GREYHOUND FORMULA Casey, Dan
£12.95 40 pb Dan Casey
Shows how to combine 10 major factors to isolate top
choices. Emphasis on grade changes, trap advantage,
early vs late speed, consistency, class and ability to stay
out of trouble. U.S. bias but still useful.
ALL LEVELS

ADVANCED HANDICAPPING RULES & REASONS
Casey, Dan
£8.95 16 pb Dan Casey
20+ ideas/angles for more experienced bettor, including
why early pace is key to finding winners, separating two
dogs of similar ability, laid off dogs chance of winning,
etc. U. S. bias.
INTERMEDIATE

CLASS RATING RACES Casey, Dan
£8.95 20 pb Dan Casey
How to use recent performance (last 3 races) to award
dogs points to assess relative merits of competing dogs.
Can be adapted for U.K. racing but U.S. bias.
ALL LEVELS

GREYHOUND GOLD Chen, J. Y.
£17.95 114 pb J. Y. Chen
Shows how to isolate bettable races while considering
key variables such as early and late pace, early pace in
long races, class, racing characteristics, trap position and
form. U.S. bias but v. good for serious punter.
INTERMEDIATE/ADVANCED

WINNING CONSISTENTLY AT THE GREYHOUND RACES Clarkin, J. J.
0934650136 £6.95 32 pb Sunnyside Publishers
Comprehensive and compact guide to U.S. Version with
an examination of how to bet, handicap, read the track
and the racecard. Covers class, early and late speed,
consistency and style and money management. U.S. bias.
BASIC

GREYHOUND RACING Coleman, Dan
£8.95 90 pb DGM
More for the novice: covers how greyhound is likely to
perform, analysing past performance records and how to
assess systems and methods. Includes thorough analysis
of class, early/late pace and running characteristics.
ALL LEVELS

GREYHOUND RACING FOR PROFIT Connolly, Liam
0900611413 £2.95 48 ST raceform
Shows how to understand grading system, value of
winning times, nine key factors for winner finding and
how to work out a successful betting strategy. Suggests
which tracks offer best chance of success.
ALL LEVELS

GREYHOUND DERBY: FIRST 60 YEARS Dack, Barrie
0948955368 £14.95 224 hb Ringpress
Comprehensive history of the richest greyhound race
this side of the Atlantic. Tells the stories of the dogs
and the people involved and the money spent in trying
to purchase a winner! B & W photos.
ALL LEVELS

GONE TO THE DOGS Duval, Ron
£12.95 65 pb Duval
Good book for beginners with excellent race examples,
points to watch when marking racecard, understand the
importance of class, running characteristics, early pace,
trap position. U.S. bias but still useful.
ALL LEVELS

WIN AT GREYHOUND RACING Edwards Clarke, H.
0948353643 £5.95 176 pb Oldcastle
Latest updated edition of one of the few books, dedicated
to finding winners. Covers winner finding on class, fitness,
family, form and shows how to assess a greyhound, a
track and how to read and analyse a race.
ALL LEVELS

IRISH GREYHOUND REVIEW 1991 Fortune, Michael
0332-3536 £7 144 pb IGR
Complete review of the 1990 Irish greyhound racing
year both track and coursing, with articles on major
races, British scene, profiles, breeding, twelve to follow,
etc.
ALL LEVELS

N.G.R.C. BOOK OF GREYHOUND RACING
Genders, Roy
072071804X £20 340 hb Pelham
Updated and revised edition of the encyclopedia of
Greyhound Racing. Over 60 B and W photos, arranged
alphabetically for easy reference.
ALL LEVELS

GREYHOUNDS Genders, Roy
9999999986 £2.95 104 hb Foyles
First published 1960 this hardback book now represents
fantastic value with both B & W and colour photos. A
little dated but still covers all the essentials of owning,
racing and the breeding of greyhounds.
ALL LEVELS

GREYHOUND STUD BOOK 1990 — Vol. 109 GSB
9999999998 £15 620 hb GSB
Yearly stud book containing overviews of Irish and British
racing year both track and field, breeding articles stud
dog tables, extended pedigrees and full list of greyhound
registered during year. Excellent production.
ALL LEVELS

GREYHOUND "YARDSTICK" 1991 Gundry-White, G.
9999999985 £3 2 Greyhound Breeders Forum
Provides accurate basis for comparing performances over
varying distances from other tracks when meeting for
first time over local distance. Hints on use are included.
If you are serious about greyhounds BUY IT!
ALL LEVELS

GREYHOUND BETTING FOR PROFIT Hamilton, Ross
0896507254 £7.95 64 pb GBC
Excellent method of handicapping for novice and more
advanced punter. Factors covered include trap position,
early speed, consistency, class. Recently updated. U.S.
bias but still useful
BASIC/INTERMEDIATE

WINNING CONSISTENTLY AT THE GREYHOUND RACES Clarkin, J. J.
0934650136 £6.95 32 pb Sunnyside Publishers
Comprehensive and compact guide to U.S. Version with an examination of how to bet, handicap, read the track and the racecard. Covers class, early and late speed, consistency and style and money management. U.S. bias.
BASIC

GREYHOUND RACING Coleman, Dan
£8.95 90 pb DGM
More for the novice: covers how greyhound is likely to perform, analysing past performance records and how to assess systems and methods. Includes thorough analysis of class, early/late pace and running characteristics.
ALL LEVELS

GREYHOUND RACING FOR PROFIT Connolly, Liam
0900611413 £2.95 48 ST raceform
Shows how to understand grading system, value of winning times, nine key factors for winner finding and how to work out a successful betting strategy. Suggests which tracks offer best chance of success.
ALL LEVELS

GREYHOUND DERBY: FIRST 60 YEARS Dack, Barrie
0948955368 £14.95 224 hb Ringpress
Comprehensive history of the richest greyhound race this side of the Atlantic. Tells the stories of the dogs and the people involved and the money spent in trying to purchase a winner! B & W photos.
ALL LEVELS

THE GREYHOUND TRAINER Montagu-Harrison, H.
9999999997 £5.95 256 pb Cashel Press
Although first published in 1962 it is still largely relevent
today being a text book on nutrition, rearing, schooling,
conditioning and training, plus section on treatment of
illnesses.
ADVANCED — for owners/trainers only

ALL ABOUT THE GREYHOUND Rollins, Anne
0948955252 £14.95 262 hb Ringpress
Comprehensive guide for the greyhound owner, trainer
and breeder. Covers origins of the breed, anatomy and
physiology (in great depth) and training. Essential book
for those involved in training and breeding.
ADVANCED

PLAYING THE DOGS — AND WINNING Sadie, Jim
£9.95 136 pb Sadie
Explains the basics (types of wagers, history, how to
read programme) and shows how to examine past
performances, develop handicapping methods and money
management. U.S. bias but still useful.
ALL LEVELS

GREYHOUND OPEN RACE RESULTS IN FULL 1989
Sporting Life
0901091324 £9.95 a 447 pb Sporting Life
Excellent guide to all NGRC open results, fully indexed
by dog and by track. Plus reports, views, statistics,
major 1990 fixtures. Invaluable.
INTERMEDIATE/ADVANCED

GREYHOUND OPEN RESULTS IN FULL 1990 Sporting Life
0901091405 £12.95 appx 500 pb Sporting Life
The latest edition of this invaluable guide to serious
punters. All NGRC open results, fully indexed by dog
and by track. Includes reports, views, statistics, major
1991 fixtures.
INTERMEDIATE/ADVANCED

THE DOGS TAM Marketing
£34.95 TAM
Can be used on ATARI/AMIGA/PC and aimed at
novice and expert with only limited time to rate races.
Uses Racing Post gives best value dog and reverse f/c.
Good but not all factors rated. State computer type and
disk size.
ALL LEVELS

ALL ABOUT THE RACING GREYHOUND Tompkins,
B & Heasman P.
0720717671 £14.95 170 hb Pelham
Written by two people actively involved in training they
cover such areas as: rearing puppies, schooling, training,
health and welfare, breeding, stud dogs and the racing
scene.
INTERMEDIATE/ADVANCED

THE GREYHOUND Top Dog series
0896864502 £9.95 48 hb Crestwood House
Aimed at juveniles or at very basic level and includes
tips on choosing pups and how to train and groom
greyhounds. Illustrated with colour photos.
BASIC

RACEFORM LTD Watling Street Road, Fulwood, Preston PR2 8AP
Phone: 0772 701243   Fax: 0772 703131

OLDCASTLE GREYHOUND CLUB

● You can now own a share in a string of greyhounds for just £100!

● Our first runner has achieved over a 30% win rate, including 3 open races at Wembley.

● 2nd runner @ Hackney won first race @ 7/1!

● We are aiming to purchase 4-6 greyhounds (funds permitting) to run top grade/minor open around the country and at S.I.S. tracks.

● Club information line on **0839 700 798.**

● Daily Greyhound Selection line on **0839 700 799** , plus any tips received from kennels.

● Club runs until December 31st 1991 - with NOTHING more to pay!

● In 1992 subject to enough support we will set up a new PLC to secure the long term future of the club in both Greyhound Racing and breeding.

THREE WAYS TO JOIN THE CLUB

1) FULL MEMBERSHIP costs £100, which includes free membership to Gamblers Book Services and three free gambling books to the value of £14-85. In addition at the end of 1991 you can convert your membership into shares in the new Oldcastle Greyhound Racing & Breeding Ltd, for a nominal administrative cost. Just send a cheque for £100, payable to Oldcastle Books Ltd to 18 Coleswood Rd, Harpenden, Herts, AL5 1EQ or ask for a brochure.

2) FULL MEMBERSHIP with payment by Standing Order. The cost is £17-95 per month for 6 months. (Total Cost £107-70). Just send a cheque (details above) for £17-95 as first payment, indicating you are taking up S/O option and we will return S/O form for you to fill out and return to us. All the benefits of full membership apply.

3) If you feel you want to be involved in the club but don't want to pay £100 and don't feel you need the benefits, full membership brings, you can subscribe as an ASSOCIATE MEMBER for just a once off payment of £20. We will give full details of the conversion of the club to company status, but you will have to subscribe for shares like everybody else, but you will have had the benefit of the club for a period and know how it works. Once again payments by cheque please for £20 to Oldcastle Books Ltd, 18 Coleswood Rd, Harpenden, Herts, AL5 1EQ

NAME :

ADDRESS :

POSTCODE :

TEL No :

Option :   1   2   3   (*Please circle your choice*)

I enclose cheque for £ _ _ _ _ _ payable to Oldcastle Books Ltd

Please send completed form to Oldcastle Greyhound Club, 18 Coleswood Rd, Harpenden, Herts AL5 1EQ

ORDER FORM

Ordering Procedure :

1) Enter titles of the books you want, their reference number, the quantity of each title required and the price extension. (See overleaf).

2) Total the price at bottom and add 10% as a contribution to P&P within the U.K., 15% if order is to go to Europe (this includes Eire) and 20% if elsewhere.

3) Send cheque, P.O. payable to Oldcastle Books Ltd or quote ACCESS/VISA number and expiry date. All payments in £ sterling.

4) Send completed form to G.B.S., Oldcastle Books Ltd, 18 Coleswood Rd, Harpenden, Herts, AL5 1EQ. You can Fax Credit Card orders on (0582) 761264.

5) Please allow up to 28 days for delivery within the U.K. & Europe, longer elsewhere. We aim to dispatch same day and of course this means you will get the book much quicker than 28 days, but at busy times and over public holidays etc, delays can occur. If a book is out of stock for a considerable period we will give you the option of cancelling your order.

— —

NAME :

ADDRESS :   POSTCODE :

Method of Payment : Cheque   P.O.   Visa   Access   (*Please circle your choice*)

Credit Card No :   _ _ _ _   _ _ _ _   _ _ _ _   _ _ _ _

Expiry date :   /   Signature :

ORDER FORM

Qty	Ref No	Book	Unit Cost	Total Cost
1)				
2)				
3)				
4)				
5)				
6)				
7)				
8)				
9)				
10)				

		Sub Total	£
		P&P	£
		NET TOTAL	£

Software Title	Type of Computer				Disk Size		Unit Cost	Total Cost
	PC	Amiga	Atari	Other	3 ½"	5 ¼"		
1)								
2)								
3)								

		Sub Total	£
		P&P	£
		NET TOTAL	£